Comparing Federal Systems in the 1990s

Ronald L. Watts

Institute of
Intergovernmental
Relations

Queen's University
Kingston, Ontario
Canada K7L 3N6

Canadian Cataloguing in Publication Data

Watts, Ronald L.
  Comparing federal systems in the 1990s

Includes bibliographical references.
ISBN 0-88911-589-3

1. Federal government. 2. Comparative government. I. Queen's University
(Kingston, Ont.). Institute of Intergovernmental Relations. II. Title.

JC355.W28 1996   321.02   C96-932464-2

Contents

List of Tables

Foreword

For many observers, the Canadian debate over the reform of our federal system has fallen into predictable patterns. Decades of argument about the central issues facing the federation seem to have etched deep grooves in our collective consciousness, subtly guiding successive rounds of discussion along familiar — and unsuccessful — lines. Yet, as Ron Watts emphasizes, Canadian debates underestimate the wonderful flexibility inherent in the central idea of federalism and the rich variety of federal arrangements that exist around the world. The central message of his monograph is that a comparative perspective can expand our understanding of the possibilities before us.

To broaden our vision, Professor Watts draws on his unique breadth of knowledge of federal systems. He explores the complexities of federations in advanced industrial nations such as the United States, Switzerland, Australia, Austria and Germany, multilingual federations such as India and Malaysia, emerging federations such as Belgium and Spain, and federations that have failed such as Czechoslovakia and Pakistan. In exploring this diverse set of countries, he focuses on the ways in which they cope with the kinds of tensions that dominate Canadian headlines every day.

Ron Watts is Principal Emeritus and Professor Emeritus of Political Studies at Queen's University, and is a Fellow of the Institute of Intergovernmental Relations. He has devoted a lifetime of study to the comparative analysis of federal systems, and is an international leader in the field. He has also served as an advisor to governments on many occasions. In 1978-79, he was a Commissioner on the Task Force on Canadian Unity (the Pepin-Robarts Commission); and in 1991-92, he served the federal government as Assistant Secretary to Cabinet for Federal-Provincial Relations (Constitutional Affairs). Since 1991 he has been President of the International Association of Centres for Federal Studies.

The Institute of Intergovernmental Relations, which is the only centre dedicated exclusively to federal studies in Canada, provides a forum for research and debate over critical questions confronting the Canadian and other federations. This study is part of the Institute's series of research monographs that examines a broad range of issues on federalism and is a companion piece to the recent study by Peter M. Leslie, *The Maastricht Model: A Canadian Perspective on the European Union*. All contributions to this series are peer reviewed.

The research for this publication was supported by the Privy Council Office of the Government of Canada. However, the views expressed are those of the author and do not necessarily represent those of the Government of Canada or the Institute of Intergovernmental Relations.

Harvey Lazar
Director
January 1997

Preface and Summary

Many observers have noted that we appear to be in the midst of a paradigm shift from a world of sovereign nation-states to a world of diminished state sovereignty and increased interstate linkages of a constitutionally federal character. Indeed there are at present twenty-three countries encompassing over 40 percent of the world's population that exhibit the fundamental characteristics of a federation. A distinctive feature about this current popularity of federalism in the world is that the application of the federal idea has taken an enormous variety of forms and that there have emerged new and innovative variants.

At a time when the future of the Canadian federation is very much in question, there would seem to be a value in looking at the theory and operation of federal systems elsewhere in the world for both the positive and the negative lessons they may provide us. All too often in the Canadian debate, it is assumed that the choice before us is limited to either the present structure of the Canadian federation, possibly adjusted by some tinkering but retaining its current structure, or the separation of a sovereign Quebec. To limit consideration to these two alternatives is to deny the potential for a multitude of possible federal arrangements, not to mention innovations, that experience elsewhere indicates can be developed within the scope of federal principles. The purpose of this study is to examine significant features of other contemporary federations to broaden our understanding of the wide range of possibilities that exist in the application of federal principles.

For this purpose a selected group of eleven other contemporary federations has been chosen for comparison. They have been chosen for their particular relevance to issues that are currently prominent in Canada and for the lessons they may provide. Four categories of federations have been selected. The first is that of federations in developed industrial societies including the United States (1789), Switzerland (1848), Australia (1901), Austria (1920), and Germany (1949). The second category consists of two federations in developing societies which, in spite of all their problems, have had a remarkable record of accommodating their intensely multilingual, multicultural and multiracial populations: India (1950) and

Malaysia (1963). The third category is represented by two recently emerged and emerging federations in developed industrial societies; Belgium (1993) and Spain (1978). These two have adopted innovative approaches to the application of the federal idea: the former in relation to bicommunal arrangements and the latter in terms of an asymmetrical approach to accommodating its Autonomous Communities. The fourth category consists of two bicommunal federations that have failed, Czechoslovakia and Pakistan, providing insights into the pathology of federations.

The introductory chapter considers some broad issues including the relevance and limits of comparative studies, the history of federalism and its particular relevance in the 1990s, conceptual issues relating to the notion of federalism, and identification of issues in the design and operation of federations.

The second chapter provides a brief overview of the 11 federations considered in this study along with Canada and outlines the distinctive features of each.

The third chapter examines how the objective of balancing unity and diversity within different federal societies has been reflected in the internal distribution of constitutional powers. It examines the relationship of legislative and of executive responsibilities to each other, and the variations in both the form of distribution of powers and the scope of responsibilities assigned to each arena of government in different federations. This is supported by an analysis in tabular form in Appendix A. A pattern that emerges is the great variety among federations, both in the form and in the allocation of specific responsibilities in them.

Chapter 4 focuses upon the distribution of financial resources within federations. This is an important aspect since it enables or constrains what the different arenas of government within each federation can do in exercising their constitutionally assigned legislative and executive responsibilities. The allocation of revenues and expenditures in different federations is compared. This indicates the virtually inevitable existence of vertical and horizontal imbalances between them and the need for intergovernmental transfers to correct these. There is considerable variation in the extent to which conditional or unconditional transfers are employed and in the use of schemes of equalization transfers. An important aspect considered as well is the processes and institutions used for adjusting the financial arrangements and the variety of forms that these have taken.

The processes that federations have adopted for achieving more general flexibility and adjustment through intergovernmental collaboration are considered in Chapter 5. It includes a consideration of the relative merits of cooperative and competitive federalism and their implications for democratic accountability. It would appear that a blend of intergovernmental cooperation and competition is in the long run the most desirable.

The issue of symmetry and asymmetry among the constituent units within a federation is addressed in Chapter 6. A distinction is made between political asymmetry and constitutional asymmetry among the constituent units within a federation and examples of each are identified. In some federations constitutional asymmetry, or at least the advocacy of it, has induced counter-pressures for symmetry suggesting that there may be limits beyond which extreme asymmetry may become dysfunctional. Nevertheless, in a number of federations the recognition of some significant constitutional asymmetry has provided an effective way of accommodating major differences in the interests and pressures for autonomy among constituent units.

A notable feature of the contemporary world is the membership of a number of federations within even wider federal organizations. Chapter 7, therefore, considers the significance of multilevel federal systems resulting from the increasing emphasis both upon supra-federation organizations and upon the role of local governments.

Chapter 8 assesses the degrees of centralization and non-centralization in different federations. While identifying the conceptual problems inherent in attempting to measure relative decentralization and autonomy, compared to other federations Canada in terms of a number of specific indices, appears to be more centralized in some aspects and more decentralized in others. In overall terms, Canada is one of the more decentralized federations although not the most.

The representative institutions of federal governments are compared in Chapter 9 with particular attention given to the difference between those based on the principle of the separation of powers and those which, like Canada, are based on the fusion of the executive and the legislature through the adoption of responsible parliamentary executives. These differences have affected the particular character of intergovernmental relations, the processes for giving voice to regional interests in federal policy making, the character of their political parties, and the role of federal second chambers.

A characteristic feature of federations generally is an emphasis upon constitutional supremacy as the ultimate source defining federal and state or provincial jurisdiction. A number of issues relating to the status of constitutions within federations are considered in Chapter 10 including the status of their constitutions as supreme law, the processes of judicial review and the role of the courts, constitutional amendment procedures, the role of constitutional bills of rights, and constitutional provisions for secession.

Chapter 11 turns to the pathology of federations. It includes an examination of the sources of stress in federations and the special problem of bicommunal federations with particular reference to the failures of Czechoslovakia and Pakistan. The chapter also gives consideration to the processes and consequences of the disintegration of federations. It notes that where separation occurs, despite professions in advance about the desirability of continued economic linkages after separation, in practice emotions aroused at the time of separation have usually meant that for a considerable subsequent period economic ties have fallen far below expectations.

The concluding chapter reviews the Canadian federation in comparison to the various other federations considered in the study, and it goes on to consider implications for the future development of the Canadian federation. These include the importance of public acceptance of the basic values and processes required for federal systems to operate effectively: explicit recognition of multiple identities and loyalties, and an overarching sense of shared purposes and objectives. Important also is a recognition of the enormous variety of ways that the federal idea can be applied to meet particular conditions, and the value of proceeding by pragmatic and incremental adjustments. Rigid and unbending federations that fail to make the substantial adjustments necessary in changing circumstances, however, are prone to crack and disintegrate.

Ronald L. Watts
December 1996

Acknowledgements

I would especially like to thank John McLean for invaluable research assistance especially in the preparation of the financial data and Appendix A. Douglas Brown read earlier drafts and provided helpful comments, as did James Hurley and David Péloquin. I am also grateful to Patti Candido and Mary Kennedy for their assistance even to the extent of interrupting vacation time.

Ronald L. Watts
December 1996

Chapter 1

Introduction

1.1 THE RELEVANCE OF COMPARISONS

In the 1990s, when the future of the Canadian federation is in question, it is instructive to look at the theory and application of federal systems that now exist elsewhere in the world. Generally speaking, Canadians have emphasized the uniqueness of their own political experience and been reluctant to undertake comparative analyses. Many Canadians seem to think of comparative studies as simply excuses for foreign travel by self-indulgent members of Parliament and sabbatical scholars or as a shameful acceptance of the pretensions of foreigners. Furthermore, the largest portion of Canadian comparative federal studies have focused on our obvious closest neighbour to the south, although there are other federations which, because of their parliamentary institutions or sociocultural and ethnic diversity, may be more usefully compared to the Canadian federation. This study, therefore, aims to survey comparatively the operation of a selected number of significant federal systems in the 1990s.

At the outset it should be noted that the comparision of federations requires some caution. There is no single pure model of federation that is applicable everywhere. Rather the basic notion of involving the combination of shared-rule for some purposes and regional self-rule for others within a single political system so that neither is subordinate to the other has been applied in different ways to fit different circumstances. Federations have varied and continue to vary in many ways: in the character and significance of the underlying economic and social diversities; in the number of constituent units and the degree of symmetry or asymmetry in their size, resources and constitutional status; in the scope of the allocation of legislative, executive and expenditure responsibilities; in the allocation of taxing power and resources; in the character of federal government institutions and the degree of regional input to federal policy making; in procedures for resolving conflicts and facilitating collaboration between interdependent governments; and in procedures for formal and informal adaptation and change.

One cannot, therefore, just pick models off a shelf. Even where similar institutions are adopted, different circumstances may make them operate differently. A classic illustration of this is the operation of the similar formal constitutional amendment procedures in Switzerland and in Australia. Both involve referendums for ratification of constitutional amendments requiring double majorities, i.e., a majority of the federal population and majorities in a majority of the constituent units. In Switzerland over 110 formal constitutional amendments have met this requirement since 1891 (over three-quarters of those initiated by Parliament and submitted to referendum), but in Australia of 42 attempts since 1901 only 8 have succeeded.

As long as these cautions are kept in mind, there is a genuine value in undertaking comparative analyses. Indeed, many of the problems we face in Canada are common to virtually all federations. Comparisons may therefore help us in several ways. They may help to identify options that might otherwise be overlooked. They may allow us to foresee more clearly the consequences of particular arrangements advocated. Through identifying similarities and difference they may draw attention to certain features of our own arrangements whose significance might otherwise be underestimated. Furthermore, comparisons may suggest both positive and negative lessons; we can learn not only from the successes but also from the failures of other federations and of the mechanisms and processes they have employed to deal with problems.

1.2 A BRIEF HISTORY OF FEDERALISM

While the United States, which adopted a federal constitution in 1787, is often regarded as the first modern federation, the history of federalism is much older.

The first documented federal system came into being among the ancient Israelite tribes over 3200 years ago.[1] Of similar antiquity were the confederations of the Bedouin tribes and the Native confederacies in North America. The early leagues of the Hellenic city-states in what is today Greece and Asia Minor were designed to aggregate communal democracies to foster trade and secure defence.[2] The Roman Republic established asymmetrical arrangements whereby Rome became the federate power and weaker cities were attached to it as federal partners.[3]

The medieval period saw self-governing cities in what is now northern Italy and Germany, and cantons in Switzerland linked in loose confederations for trade and defence purposes. The Swiss confederation established in 1291 lasted despite some disruptions until 1847. In the late sixteenth century an independent confederation, the United Provinces of the Netherlands, was established during a revolt against Spain. Both the Swiss and Netherlands confederations were affected by the Reformation which sharpened internal divisions. This period also saw the first writing on explicitly federal theory, exemplified by the *Politica Methodice Digesta* of Althusius and subsequently by the efforts of German theorists to provide a grounding for a restored and modernized Holy Roman Empire. Several of the British settlements in North America, particularly in New England, were based on federal arrangements growing out of Reformed Protestantism.

Following the American Revolution the newly independent states established a confederation in 1781. Its deficiencies, however, led to its transformation in 1789, following the Philadelphia Convention of 1787, into the first modern federation. Switzerland, after a brief civil war, transformed its confederation into a federation in 1848. Canada became the third modern federation in 1867. Not long after, in 1901, Australia became a full-fledged federation. In addition, during the latter part of the nineteenth century and the early twentieth century a number of Latin American republics adopted federal structures in imitation of the U.S. federation.

The second half of the twentieth century has seen a proliferation of federations as well as other federal forms to unite multi-ethnic communities in former colonial areas and in Europe. New federations or quasi-federations, not all of which have survived, were founded in Asia, for example, in Indochina (1945), Burma (1948), Indonesia (1949), India (1950), Pakistan (1956), Malaya (1948 and 1957) and then Malaysia (1963); in the Middle East, e.g. in the United Arab Emirates (1971); in Africa, e.g. Libya (1951), Ethiopia (1952), Rhodesia and Nyasaland (1953), Nigeria (1954), Mali (1959), the Congo (1960), Cameroon (1961), and Comoros (1978); and in the Caribbean, e.g. the West Indies (1958). Among the federations founded or restored in central and eastern Europe were those of Austria (1945), Yugoslavia (1946), Germany (1949) and Czechoslovakia (1970). In South America, Brazil (1946), Venezuela (1947) and Argentina (1949) adopted new federal constitutions.

Between 1960 and the late 1980s, however, it became increasingly clear that federal systems were not the panacea that many had imagined them to be. Many of the post-war federal experiments experienced difficulties and a number of them were temporarily suspended or abandoned outright. These experiences suggested that, even when undertaken with the best of motives there are limits to the appropriateness of federal solutions or particular federal forms in certain circumstances.

Despite these developments there has been a revival of interest in federal political solutions in the 1990s. Belgium (1993), South Africa (1996) and Spain (which as a result of the operation of the 1978 constitution has in practice become a federation in all but name) have been moving towards new federal and quasi-federal forms. In Italy too there has been pressure for the adoption of a federal system. Progress towards greater integration in what has become the European Union has also heightened interest in federal ideas. Political leaders, leading intellectuals and even some journalists increasingly refer to federalism as a liberating and positive form of political organization.

1.3 THE RELEVANCE OF FEDERALISM IN THE 1990s

Federalism is far from being an obsolete nineteenth century form of government inappropriate in the contemporary world. In fact, in the last decade it is the concept of the nation-state, developed in the seventeenth century, that more and more people have been coming to regard as obsolete. Observers have noted that we appear to be in the midst of a paradigm shift which is taking us from a world of sovereign nation-states to a world of diminished state sovereignty and increased interstate linkages of a constitutionally federal character. There are, at present, 23 federations containing about two billion people or 40 percent of the world population; they encompass about 480 constituent or federated states compared to only approximately 180 politically sovereign states. In addition to these federations, there have emerged new variants in the application of the federal idea. Just one of many examples is the European Union where individual federations, unions and unitary states have "pooled their sovereignty" (as they express it) in a hybrid structure which has come to involve elements of confederation and federation.

There are a number of reasons for this international trend to increased pooling of sovereignty among states in various federal forms. First, modern developments in transportation, social communications, technology and industrial organization have produced pressures at one and the same time for larger political organizations and for smaller ones. The pressure for larger political units has been generated by the goals shared by most Western and non-Western societies today: a desire for progress, a rising standard of living, social justice, and influence in the world arena, and by a growing awareness of world-wide interdependence in an era whose advanced technology makes both mass destruction and mass construction possible. The desire for smaller, self-governing political units has risen from the desire to make governments more responsive to the individual citizen and to give expression to primary group attachments — linguistic and cultural ties, religious connections, historical traditions and social practices — which provide the distinctive basis for a community's sense of identity and yearning for self-determination. Given these dual pressures throughout the world, more and more peoples have come to see some form of federalism, combining a shared government for specified common purposes with autonomous action by constituent units of government for purposes related to maintaining their regional distinctiveness, as allowing the closest institutional approximation to the multinational reality of the contemporary world.

Second, and closely related, is the recognition that an increasingly global economy has itself unleashed economic and political forces strengthening both international *and* local pressures at the expense of the traditional nation-state. Global communications and consumership have awakened desires in the smallest and most remote villages around the world for access to the global marketplace of goods and services. As a result, governments have been faced increasingly with the desires of their people to be both *global* consumers and *local* citizens at the same time. Tom Courchene has labelled this trend "glocalization."[4] Thus, the nation-state itself is simultaneously proving both too small and too large to serve all the desires of its citizens. Because of the development of the world market economy, the old-fashioned nation-state can no longer deliver many of the benefits its citizens value, such as rising living standards and job security. Self-sufficiency of the nation-state is widely recognized as unattainable and nominal sovereignty is less appealing if it means that, in reality, people have less control over decisions that crucially affect them. At the same time, nation-states have come to be too remote from individual citizens to provide a sense of direct democratic control and to respond clearly to the specific concerns and preferences of their citizens. In such a context federalism with its different interacting levels of government has provided a way of mediating the variety of global and local citizen preferences.

Third, the spread of market-based economies is creating socioeconomic conditions conducive to support for the federal idea. Among these are the emphasis on contractual relationships; the recognition of the non-centralized character of a market-based economy; entrepreneurial self-governance and consumer rights consciousness; markets that thrive on diversity rather than homogeneity, on interjurisdictional mobility and on competition as well as cooperation; and the recognition that people do not have to like each other in order to benefit each other.

Fourth, changes in technology have been generating new and more federal models of industrial organization with decentralized and "flattened hierarchies" involving non-centralized interactive networks. This in turn has produced more favourable attitudes towards non-centralized political organization.

Fifth, increasing public attention, especially in Europe, has been given to the principle of "subsidiarity," the notion that a "higher" political body should take up only those tasks that cannot be accomplished by the "lower" political bodies themselves. There are some problems in the concept: it is difficult to translate it into legal terms, it has a clearly hierarchical character, and it implies that ultimately it is for the "higher" body to decide at which level tasks should be performed. Nevertheless, the decentralist thrust of the subsidiarity principle has been instrumental in encouraging wider interest in a "citizen-oriented federalism."

Yet another factor has been the resilience of the classical federations in the face of changing conditions. The constitutions of the United States (1789), Switzerland (1848), Canada (1867) and Australia (1901) are among the longest-surviving of any in the world today. In spite of problems experienced over the past three decades, these four federations along with Germany, another federation, have displayed a degree of flexibility and adaptability; they place high in international rankings of the most desirable countries in which to live.

For all these reasons, the federal idea is now more popular internationally than at any time in history. This suggests that Canadians should be wary of rejecting the advantages that so many elsewhere see in federal solutions.

A distinctive feature about the current popularity of federalism in the world is that the application of the federal idea has taken a great variety of forms. The degrees of centralization or decentralization differ across federations as do their financial arrangements, the character of their federal legislative and executive institutions, institutional arrangements for facilitating intergovernmental relations, judicial arrangements for umpiring internal conflicts, and procedures for constitutional amendment. Among interesting recent developments and innovations has been the acceptance in an increasing number of instances of some degree of asymmetry in the relationship of member units to federations or to supranational organizations. Examples in practice include Belgium, Malaysia, Russia, Spain and, following the Maastricht Treaty, the European Union. Another has been the trend for federations themselves to become constituent members of even wider federations or supranational organizations. Examples are Germany, Belgium and now Austria within the European Union.[5] It is also worth noting that the three members of the North American Free Trade Agreement (NAFTA), Canada, the USA and Mexico are each themselves federations. Thus there has been an emerging trend towards three or even four (not just two) levels of federal organization to reconcile supranational, national, regional and local impulses in order to maximize the realization of citizen preferences.

All this suggests that to assume that a sovereign Quebec is the only alternative to the current structure of the Canadian federation is to deny the potential for a multitude of variations, not to mention innovations, that could be developed in the process of the political evolution of the Canadian federation. The choice is not necessarily limited to "federation or sovereignty" but encompasses a variety of possible relationships towards which the Canadian federation might evolve as a result of either non-constitutional political adaptation or constitutional adjustment or both.

1.4 DEFINITION OF TERMS AND PRINCIPLES OF FEDERALISM

There has been much scholarly debate about the definition of federalism. For the sake of clarity we may distinguish three terms: "federalism," "federal political systems," and "federations." "Federalism" is basically not a descriptive but a normative term and refers to the advocacy of multi-tiered government combining elements of shared-rule and regional self-rule. It is based on the presumed value and validity of combining unity and diversity and of accommodating, preserving and promoting distinct identities within a larger political union. The essence of federalism as a normative principle is the perpetuation of both union and non-centralization at the same time.

"Federal political systems" and "federations" are descriptive terms applying to particular forms of political organization. The term "federal political system" refers to a broad category of political systems in which, by contrast to the single central source of authority in unitary systems, there are two (or more) levels of government which combine elements of *shared-rule* through common institutions and *regional self-rule* for the governments of the constituent units. This broad genus encompasses a whole spectrum of more specific non-unitary forms, i.e. species, ranging from "quasi-federations" and "federations" to "confederacies" and beyond. Indeed, Daniel Elazar has identified the following as specific categories: unions, constitutionally decentralized unions, federations, confederations, federacies, associated statehood, condominiums, leagues and joint functional authorities.[6] (See Table 1 for definitions of these terms.) Tables 2, 3, 4, 5 and 6 list current examples of federal forms.[7] Furthermore, other political systems outside the general category of federal systems may incorporate some federal arrangements because political leaders and nation-builders are less bound by considerations of theoretical purity than by the pragmatic search for workable political arrangements. Such considerations may also lead to hybrids such as the European Union which, although originally a purely confederal arrangement, has in recent years been moving towards incorporating some features of a federation.

Within the genus of federal political systems, federations represent a particular species in which neither the federal nor the constituent units of government are constitutionally subordinate to the other, i.e. each has sovereign powers derived from the constitution rather than another level of government, each is empowered to deal directly with its citizens in the exercise of its legislative, executive and taxing powers and each is directly elected by its citizens. Table 2 identifies 23 contemporary examples not including the embryonic Croat-Muslim federation of Bosnia.

The generally common structural characteristics of federations as a specific form of federal political system are the following:

- two orders of government each acting directly on their citizens;
- a formal constitutional distribution of legislative and executive authority and allocation of revenue resources between the two orders of government ensuring some areas of genuine autonomy for each order;
- provision for the designated representation of distinct regional views within the federal policy-making institutions, usually provided by the particular form of the federal second chamber;
- a supreme written constitution not unilaterally amendable and requiring the consent of a significant proportion of the constituent units;
- an umpire (in the form of courts or provision for referendums) to rule on disputes between governments;
- processes and institutions to facilitate intergovernmental collaboration for those areas where governmental responsibilities are shared or inevitably overlap.

TABLE 1:   The Spectrum of Federal Political Systems

Unions	polities compounded in such a way that the constituent units preserve their respective integrities primarily or exclusively through the common organs of the general government rather than through dual government structures. New Zealand and Lebanon are examples. Belgium prior to becoming a federation in 1993 was an example (when central legislators served also with a dual mandate as regional or community councillors).
Constitutionally decentralized unions	basically unitary in form in the sense that ultimate authority rests with the central government but incorporate constitutionally protected subnational units of government which have functional autonomy. See Table 5 for examples.
Federations	compound polities, combining strong constituent units and a strong general government, each possessing powers delegated to it by the people through a constitution, and each empowered to deal directly with the citizens in the exercise of its legislative, administrative and taxing powers, and each directly elected by the citizens. Currently there are some 23 federations in the world. See Table 2 for examples.
Confederations	These occur where several pre-existing polities join together to form a common government for certain limited purposes (for foreign affairs, defence or economic purposes), but the common government is dependent upon the constituent governments, being composed of delegates from the constituent governments and therefore having only an indirect electoral and fiscal base. Historical examples have been Switzerland for most of the period 1291-1847 and the United States 1776-89. In the contemporary world, the European Union is primarily a confederation although it has increasingly incorporated some features of a federation. See Table 3 for other examples.
Federacies	political arrangements where a large unit is linked to a smaller unit or units, but the smaller unit retains considerable autonomy and has a minimum role in the government of the larger one, and where the relationship can be dissolved only by mutual agreement. Examples are the relationship of Puerto Rico to the United States and of Bhutan to India. See Table 4 for other examples.
Associated states	These relationships are similar to federacies, but they can be dissolved by either of the units acting alone on prearranged terms. Examples are the relationships between the United States and the Marshall Islands, and between New Zealand and the Cook Islands. See Table 4 for other examples.

... continued

TABLE 1 *(continued)*

Condominiums	political units which function under the joint rule of two or more external states in such a way that the inhabitants have substantial internal self-rule. An example is Andorra which functioned under the joint rule of France and Spain 1278-1993.
Leagues	linkages of politically independent polities for specific purposes that function through a common secretariat rather than a government and from which members may unilaterally withdraw. See Table 6 for examples.
Joint functional authorities	An agency established by two or more polities for joint implementation of a particular task or tasks. The North Atlantic Fisheries Organization (NAFO), the International Atomic Energy Agency (IAEA) and the International Labour Organization (ILO) are three of many examples. Such joint functional authorities may also take the form of transborder organizations established by adjoining sub-national governments, e.g. the interstate grouping for economic development involving four regions in Italy, four Austrian Länder, two Yugoslav republics and one West German Land established in 1978, and the interstate Regio Basiliensis involving Swiss, German and French co-operation in the Basle area.
Hybrids	Some political systems combine characteristics of different kinds of political systems. Examples are Canada initially in 1867 which was basically a federation but contained some quasi-unitary elements; more recently, South Africa (1996), which is a federation retaining some quasi-unitary features; and the European Union after Maastricht which is basically a confederation but has some features of a federation. Hybrids occur because statesmen are often more interested in pragmatic political solutions than in theoretical purity.

TABLE 2:   Contemporary Federations

Name (Constituent Units)

Argentine Republic (23 provinces + 5 regions + 1 national territory + 1 federal district)

Commonwealth of Australia (6 states + 1 territory + 1 capital territory + 7 administered territories)

Federal Republic of Austria (9 *Länder*)

Belgium (3 regions + 3 cultural communities)

Brazil (26 states + 1 federal capital district)

Canada (10 provinces + 2 territories + Aboriginal organizations)

The Federal and Islamic Republic of the Comoros (3 islands)

Ethiopia (9 provinces)

Federal Republic of Germany (16 *Länder*)

Republic of India (25 states + 7 union territories + 1 federacy + 1 associated state)

Malaysia (13 states)

United Mexican States (31 states + 1 federal district)

Federal Republic of Nigeria (30 states + 1 federal capital territory)

Islamic Republic of Pakistan (4 provinces + 6 tribal areas + 1 federal capital)

Russian Federation (89 republics and various categories of regions)

St. Kitts and Nevis (2 islands)

South Africa (9 provinces)

Spain (17 autonomous regions)

Swiss Confederation (26 cantons)

United Arab Emirates (7 emirates)

United States of America (50 states + 2 federacies + 3 associated states + 3 local home-rule territories + 3 unincorporated territories + 130 Native American domestic dependent nations)

Republic of Venezuela (20 states + 2 territories + 1 federal district + 2 federal dependencies + 72 islands)

Federal Republic of Yugoslavia (2 republics)

TABLE 3:   Contemporary Confederations

Name (Constituent Units)
Benelux (3 member states)
Caribbean Community (14 member states + 2 associate members + 6 observers)
Commonwealth of Independent States (12 member states)
European Union (15 member states)

TABLE 4:   Associated States, Federacies and Condominiums

Name (Form)	*Federated Power*
Aaland Islands (federacy)	Finland
Andorra (condominium)	France and Spain
Azores Islands (federacy)	Portugal
Bhutan (associated state)	India
Cook Islands (associated state)	New Zealand
Faroe Islands (federacy)	Denmark
Federated States of Micronesia (associated state)	United States
Greenland (federacy)	Denmark
Gurnsey (federacy)	United Kingdom
Isle of Man (federacy)	United Kingdom
Jammu and Kashmir (federacy)	India
Jersey (federacy)	United Kingdom
Liechtenstein (associated state)	Switzerland
Macao (associated state)	Portugal
Madeira Islands (federacy)	Portugal
Marshall Islands (associated state)	United States
Monaco (associated state)	France
Netherlands Antilles (associated state)	Netherlands
Niue Island (associated state)	New Zealand
Northern Marianas (federacy)	United States
Puerto Rico (federacy)	United States
Republic of Palau (associated state)	United States
San Marino (associated state)	Italy

TABLE 5: Decentralized Unions with Some Federal Features

Name (Number of Constituent Units)

Antigua and Barbuda (2 islands)

People's Republic of China (22 provinces + 5 autonomous regions + 3 municipalities)

Colombia (23 departments + 4 intendencies + 3 commissaries)

Fiji Islands (consociation of 2 ethnic communities)

Ghana (10 regions)

Georgia (2 autonomous regions)

Indonesia (27 provinces)

Italy (15 ordinary regions + 5 autonomous regions)

Japan (47 *to-do-fu-ken*/prefectures)

Myanmar/Burma (7 states, 7 divisions)

Namibia (14 regions)

Netherlands (11 provinces + 1 associated state)

Papua New Guinea (19 provinces + 1 capital district)

Portugal (state with 2 autonomous overseas regions)

Solomon Islands (4 districts)

Sudan (6 regions + 1 federally administered province)

Tanzania (2 constituent units)

United Kingdom of Great Britain and Northern Ireland (4 countries +
    5 self-governing islands)

Ukraine (1 autonomous region)

Vanuatu (constitutionally regionalized islands)

TABLE 6: Examples of Varieties of Federal Arrangements

Decentralized Union	Federation	Confederation	Federacy	Associated Statehood	Condominium	League
Antigua-Barbuda	Argentina	Benelux Economic Union	Denmark-Faroes	France-Monaco	Andorra-France and Spain (1278-1993)	Arab League
China	Australia	Caribbean Community	Finland-Aaland	India-Bhutan		Association of South East Asian Nations (ASEAN)
Colombia	Austria	Commonwealth of Independent States	India-Kashmir	Italy-San Marino		Baltic Assembly
Italy	Belgium	European Union	Portugal-Azores	Netherlands-Netherlands Antilles		Commonwealth of Nations
Japan	Brazil		Portugal-Madeira	New Zealand-Cook Islands		North Atlantic Treaty Organization (NATO)
Netherlands	Canada		UK-Guernsey	New Zealand-Niue Islands		Nordic Council
Papua/New Guinea	Comoros		UK-Jersey	Switzerland-Liechtenstein		South Asian Association for Regional Cooperation (SAARC)
Solomon Islands	Ethiopia		UK-Man	US-Marshall Islands		
Sudan	Germany		US-Northern Marianas	US-Micronesia		
Tanzania	India		US-Puerto Rico	US-Palau		
United Kingdom	Malaysia					
Vanuatu	Mexico					
	Nigeria					
	Pakistan					
	Russia					
	South Africa					
	Spain					
	St. Kitts-Nevis					
	Switzerland					
	United Arab Emirates					
	United States					
	Venezuela					
	Yugoslavia					

There are several important points to note. First, there is an important distinction between constitutional form and operational reality. In many political systems political practice has transformed the way the constitution operates. In Canada and India, for example, the initial constitution was quasi-federal containing some central overriding powers more typical of unitary systems. But in Canada these powers have fallen into disuse and in India they have been moderated so that in both cases operational reality comes closer to that of a full-fledged federation. Other particularly notable examples of the impact of operational practice have occurred in Switzerland, Russia and Belgium. Thus, to understand federal systems generally and federations in particular it is necessary to study both their constitutional law and their politics and how they interact.

Second, while knowledge about the structural character of a federal political system or a federation is important to gain an understanding of its character, equally important is the nature of its political processes. Significant characteristics of federal processes include a strong predisposition to democracy since they presume the voluntary consent of citizens in the constituent units, non-centralization as a principle expressed through multiple centres of political decision making, open political bargaining as a major feature of the way in which decisions are arrived at, the operation of checks and balances to avoid the concentration of political power, and a respect for constitutionalism since each order of government derives its authority from the constitution.

Third, federal processes may be territorial or consociational or both. While there are some examples of federations in which there are nonterritorial constituent units recognized in the constitution, the most notable example being the Belgian Communities, the constitutional distribution of power among *territorial* units is by far the most common pattern among federations. In many federations the constitutional powers are distributed equally among the main category of constituent units but it is noteworthy that in some federations there is some asymmetry in the relationship of the main constituent units (e.g. Canada, Malaysia, India, Spain and Russia), in some the main constituent units are classified into two or more categories (e.g. Malaysia and Russia), and in many there are categories of "territories" distinguished from the major constituent units (Table 2 indicates those federations that include territories.)

1.5 ISSUES IN THE DESIGN AND OPERATION OF FEDERATIONS

This study, because its aim is to draw lessons from other federations, will focus on the following issues in the design and operation of federations:

1. The interrelation of social institutions, institutional structures and political processes and the interaction of these affecting each other. This theme, rather than being treated in a separate section, runs through all the sections of this study.

2. The common and varying features of federations

    •   the common objectives of combining unity and diversity
    •   common institutional structures and processes in federations
    •   variations in the institutional structures and processes of federations

    Consideration of the common and varying features of federations also runs through all the sections of this study.

3. Issues in the design of federations that affect their operation

    •   the character of the constituent units in terms of their number, absolute and relative sizes, and absolute and relative wealth
    •   the distribution of functions in terms of the following:

        –   the form of distribution including the significance of exclusive, concurrent (shared) and residual authority assigned to each level
        –   the allocation of legislative and administrative responsibilities
        –   the scope of functions allocated to each level
        –   the allocation of financial resources
        –   degrees of symmetry or asymmetry in the allocation of powers to constituent units
        –   structures and processes relating to intergovernmental relations within federations
        –   degrees of decentralization and non-centralization
        –   degrees of autonomy or interdependence of governments
        –   identification of commonly regarded essential federal powers

    •   the nature of the common federative institutions

        –   the distinction in this respect between federations and confederations
        –   the distinction between parliamentary and non-parliamentary federations and their differing impact
        –   special provisions for proportionate representation of constituent units in the federal executive, legislative (particularly second chambers), public service and agencies
        –   the role of constituent unit representatives in common decision making

    •   the role and status of the constitution

        –   as supreme law
        –   the role of the courts and judicial review
        –   the issue of balancing rigidity and flexibility
        –   formal constitutional amendment processes
        –   the role of referendums
        –   safeguarding individual and collective rights

1.6 CRITERIA FOR THE SELECTION OF FEDERATIONS
CONSIDERED IN THIS STUDY

This comparative study focuses primarily on federations rather than confederations since the applicability of the experience of the most significant contemporary
confederation, the European Union, has already been examined in depth recently
in a study by Peter M. Leslie.[8] Furthermore, that study focuses on federations as
more directly relevant to current deliberations in Canada rather than upon the
other more peripheral federal forms such as federacies referred to in section 1.4
above and listed in Table 1. Examples have been selected for their relevance to
issues currently under discussion in Canada, from four categories of federations.

The first category is that of federations in developed industrial societies, including the United States, Switzerland, Australia, Germany and Austria. These
are particularly relevant because they are relatively long-standing federations and
have similar economic and social circumstances. The conditions and political traditions in these federations more closely resemble those in Canada than do those
of most of the federations in developing countries in Asia, Africa or Latin America.
Furthermore, the examples selected for consideration in this study, unlike some
of the nominal federations in South America, Asia and Africa, represent true federations in which both the federal and state governments not only have formally
independent powers but exercise them in practice.

The second category is that of two federations in developing societies selected
for their particular relevance to Canada. These are India and Malaysia. Both are
multilingual, multicultural and multiracial in character. Furthermore, both like
Canada are parliamentary federations. They have a special significance because
their current federal structures were heavily influenced by the example of the
Government of India Act, 1935, which itself was modelled on the Canadian federal structure. It is worth noting that both of these federations are now more than
thirty years old, and they have exhibited surprising and unexpected stability in the
face of sharp internal diversity.

The third category is that of recently emerged and emerging federations in
developed countries, notably Belgium and Spain. In 1993 two decades of step-
by-step devolution in Belgium culminated in the implementation of an explicitly
federal constitution. In the case of Spain, the 1978 constitution has produced a
process of asymmetrical devolution which has resulted in a federation in every-
thing but name. As developed countries the economic and social conditions of
Belgium and Spain are more akin to those of Canada than are those of developing
countries. Furthermore, the bicommunal character of Belgium and the asymmetrical process of evolution in Spain are each particularly relevant for issues facing
Canada. Russia is another example in this category that might have been considered, particularly in view of the asymmetrical situation of its 89 constituent units,
but its currently fluid transitional character makes drawing conclusive lessons
based on its experience tenuous. South Africa is another example of an emergent

federation with the interim quasifederal constitution of 1994 being succeeded now by the constitution of 1996 that is broadly similar in character to the interim one. But while it exhibits many interesting features, the circumstances of South Africa are very different from those of Canada and these developments are very recent.

A fourth category, to which some attention will be paid particularly in the section on the pathology of federations, is that of the bicommunal federations of Czechoslovakia and Pakistan, both of which separated into independent successor states. The USSR and Yugoslavia provide examples of multiethnic federations that have recently disintegrated and there are other examples of federations in Africa and the Caribbean that have splintered, but for Canadians the examples of Czechoslovakia and Pakistan are the most relevant because these two federations were primarily bicommunal in character and each ultimately split into two successor states.

The federations selected for review in this study encompass a wide range of variations. Four are relatively compact federations in Europe (Switzerland, Austria, Germany and Belgium), while four cover vast continental land masses (two, Canada and the USA in North America; one on the Indian sub-continent and Australia in the South Pacific). Four (the USA, Switzerland, Canada and Australia) have existed for nearly a century or more, while four (Austria, Germany, India and Malaysia) were restored or created after World War II, and two (Belgium and Spain) are brand new. Four (Canada, Australia, India and Malaysia) have parliamentary systems on the majoritarian Westminster model, while the others, in a variety of forms, have more effective arrangements for regional representation and participation in decision making at the federal level. Six (Switzerland, India, Malaysia, Belgium, Spain and Canada) have significant territorially based minority language groups while the others are more homogeneous. Two (Pakistan and Czechoslovakia) were bicommunal federations that subsequently split in two. Thus, the federations selected for review provide a considerable variety of geographic, demographic, historical, economic, political and interterritorial characteristics from which lessons may be drawn.

Chapter 2

Overview of the Federations Compared
in this Study

For each of the federations compared in this study, this section will outline briefly its origin, evolution, underlying conditions and factors, institutional structure, distinctive political processes and major issues.

2.1 ESTABLISHED FEDERATIONS IN DEVELOPED COUNTRIES

United States of America (1789)

The United States of America, the first modern federation, adopted federation as the organizing principle for its structure of government in 1789 following the Philadelphia Convention of 1787. This resulted from the failure of a confederal form of government established under the Articles of Confederation of 1781. Originally comprised of 13 states, the United States has evolved into a federation of 50 states plus 2 federacies, 3 associated states, 3 local home-rule territories, 3 unincorporated territories and over 130 Native American domestic dependent nations. It survived a devastating civil war during the first century of its existence, but as the most enduring federation in the world, it is an important reference point in any comparative study of federations.

Among federations it is marked by a relatively homogeneous society. There are significant black and hispanic minorities but in no state do they constitute a majority. Nevertheless, there are regional variations in political culture and a considerable emphasis upon the value of state and local government.

In comparative terms the federation is moderately decentralized. Jurisdiction assigned to the 50 states is symmetrical, although this does not apply to the relationship of the various federacies and associated states. The major feature of the distribution of powers is the arrangement whereby the constitution lists subject matters under federal authority — most of which are concurrent and some of which are made exclusively federal by prohibiting the states from legislating on them — and leaves the unspecified residual matters to the states.

The federal institutions are based on the principle of the separation of powers between executive and legislature with Presidential-Congressional institutions involving a system of checks and balances. Congress includes a Senate in which the states are equally represented with members elected directly (since 1912).

Virtually all subsequently attempted federations have taken some account of the constitutional design and operation of the United States in developing their own federal structures.

Switzerland (1848)

The Swiss Confederation, which had existed in various forms since 1291, broke down in the brief Sonderbund Civil War of 1847; a new constitution in 1848 converted it into a federation. Switzerland, a small country of some 7 million people, now comprises 26 constituent units called cantons, of which 6 are designated "half cantons."

The Swiss federation is notable for its significant degree of linguistic and religious diversity, although the German Swiss continue to dominate in overall numbers and economic power. Its three official languages (German, French and Italian; a fourth, Romansh, is recognized as a "national language") and two dominant faiths (Roman Catholic and Protestant) represent territorial cleavages that cut across each other. Among German-speaking cantons, some are Roman Catholic and some are Protestant, similarly some French-speaking cantons are Roman Catholic and some are Protestant. Consequently, on different issues cantons form different alignments. Of the 26 cantons, 17 are unilingually German, 4 are unilingually French and one is Italian, 3 are bilingual German and French and one, Graubunden, is trilingual (German, Italian, Romansh). In all, 14 cantons have Roman Catholic majorities and 12 have Protestant majorities, the Roman Catholic or Protestant majorities representing more than two-thirds of the cantonal population in 18 of the 26 cantons.

While under the constitutional distribution of powers a significant proportion are assigned to the federal government with the residual powers to the cantons, there is in practice a high degree of decentralization because the constitution leaves the federal government highly dependent upon the autonomous cantons for the administration of a large portion of its legislation. There is a relative symmetry in the jurisdiction of the cantons, although 6 of the 26 cantons are classified as "half cantons" and therefore each of these has only half the representation in the Council of States (Standerat).

The principle of the separation of powers has been applied to the federal institutions but the executive (the Federal Council) is a collegial body elected by the Swiss federal legislature for a fixed term and composed of seven councillors among whom the presidency rotates annually. The federal legislature is bicameral composed of the National Council (Nationalrat) and Council of States (Standerat) and in the latter cantons have two representatives each and half cantons one. The electoral system based on proportional representation has resulted in a multiparty system, but the fixed-term executive has provided stability and the tradition has developed that it should encompass the four major political parties representing an overwhelming majority in the federal legislature. A characteristic of the Swiss political process has been the widespread use of referendums and initiatives. Another feature is that dual membership in the cantonal and federal legislatures is permitted so that about one-fifth of federal legislators are also members of cantonal legislatures.

Although small in terms of population and area, its multilingual and multicultural character make Switzerland a federation of particular relevance to Canada.

Canada (1867)

Second only to Russia in territorial size, Canada became a federation in 1867. While the term "Confederation" is used by Canadians this refers to the process of bringing provinces together into a federation in 1869 rather than the adoption of a confederal structure. The federation grew out of efforts to overcome the political difficulties and deadlocks within the United Province of Canada created by the Act of Union of 1840. This was to be achieved by splitting it into the two new provinces of Ontario with an English-speaking majority and Quebec with a French-speaking majority, and by the addition of the Maritime provinces of Nova Scotia and New Brunswick both for trade and defence purposes. Originally a union of four provinces, the federation has grown until it is now composed of ten provinces and two northern territories, which in 1999, following division of the Northwest Territories will be three. A distinctive feature of the Canadian federation is the continuing existence and vitality of a French Canadian majority concentrated within one province. Approximately 80 percent of the French Canadian population lives in Quebec where they constitute over 80 percent of the population. Throughout its history the Canadian federation has been marked both by the French-English duality and by a strong regionalism expressed through the provinces. More recently there has been increasing attention given to recognizing the place of the Aboriginal Peoples within the federation.

The original 1867 constitution was marked by strong central powers including some powers enabling the federal government to override the provinces in certain circumstances. Unlike the two federations that preceded it, the constitution designated three forms of legislative powers: exclusively federal, exclusively provincial and concurrent, with the residual powers assigned to the federal government. Despite its originally centralized form, a century and a quarter of pressures to recognize duality and regionalism have made Canada a relatively decentralized federation both legislatively and administratively. The *Constitution Act, 1867* recognized the particular character of Quebec by including some recognition of asymmetry in provisions relating to language, education and civil law. But efforts within the last three decades to recognize the reality of Quebec's distinctiveness by increasing constitutional asymmetry have been highly controversial.

The most innovative feature of the federation was that, in contrast to the U.S. and Swiss federations, which emphasized the separation of the executive and legislature in their federal institutions, Canada was the first federation to incorporate a system of parliamentary responsible government in which the executive and the legislature are fused. This combination of federal and parliamentary systems was subsequently adopted in Australia, in many of the other federations considered in this study. The majoritarian character of the parliamentary federal institutions has had a significant impact on the dynamics of federal politics in Canada.

Australia (1901)

The Australian federal constitution of 1901 united a number of self-governing British colonies. Today the federation comprises six states (of which the two most populous, New South Wales and Victoria, comprise 60 percent of the federal population) plus one capital territory, the Northern Territory, and seven administered territories.

Australia is a relatively homogeneous society with a population of about 18 million people mostly descended from British and European settlers, but the geographic vastness and concentrations of population in dispersed state capitals each serving its own hinterland have made federation a natural form of political organization.

The founders of the Australian federation rejected the Canadian model of a relatively centralized distribution of powers and followed the American model enumerating a limited list of federal exclusive powers and a substantial list of concurrent powers, and leaving unspecified residual powers to the state governments. In practice, however, the Australian federation has evolved into a relatively more centralized federation, particularly with respect to financial arrangements. In terms of jurisdiction there is a symmetry among the six states.

While adopting a different form of distribution of powers, the Australian federation did follow the Canadian precedent of combining federal and parliamentary institutions, responsible cabinet government operating at both federal and state levels. Nevertheless, it incorporated a relatively powerful directly elected senate with equal representation of the provinces. The impact of the parliamentary system has, however, made the Senate more of a "party house" than a "regional house."

As a parliamentary federation Australia has developed the institutions and processes of "executive federalism" more extensively than Canada has. With its British heritage of parliamentary institutions and tradition of executive federalism, Australia as a federation is of continuing relevance for the study of the Canadian federation.

Austria (1920)

Austria adopted a federal constitution in 1920, shortly after the demise of the Austro-Hungarian Empire. Modifications were made in 1929 and again in 1945, the Austrian Republic was restored, but the fundamental character of the original constitution remained basically unchanged. Currently, with a population of 8 million, it comprises nine Länder.

Austria is largely culturally homogeneous. German is the official language, although special constitutional provision is made for the use of the Slovene and Croat languages in certain regions of the country.

Given a statist and hierarchical traditional political culture, the Austrian federation exhibits a highly centralized legislative jurisdiction but with the administration of federal law extensively decentralized to the Länder. Among federations it is one of the most centralized with the constituent units often serving mainly as "agents" and "subordinates" of the federal government, although they are assigned the residual legislative authority. Within the federation the units are symmetrical in power and status.

Federal government institutions are parliamentary in character, the Chancellor and Cabinet being responsible to the Nationalrat, although there is a directly elected federal president who performs the functions of head of state. The federal legislature is bicameral. The members of the second chamber (the Bundesrat) are indirectly elected by the assemblies of the Länder with representation fairly closely proportional to population except for a minimum guarantee of three representatives for each Land.

The Austrian federation is of interest because it shows how far centralization and federal-state interdependence can be taken in the spectrum of federal arrangements.

Germany (1949)

The German federation owes a good deal to the Austrian precedent and also to the earlier experience of the German Empire (1871-1918), the Weimer Republic (1919-34) and the failure of the totalitarian centralization of the Third Reich (1934-45). West Germany in 1949 became the Federal Republic of Germany comprising 11 Länder. The reunification of Germany in 1990 provided for the accession of five new Länder. The federation now consists of 16 Länder with a total population of over 80 million.

The population of the German federation is linguistically homogeneous, although there remains a considerable gulf between the political cultures of the former West Germany and the former East Germany.

A notable characteristic of the German federation is the interlocked relationship of the federal and state governments. The federal government has a broad range of exclusive, concurrent and framework legislative powers, but the Länder have a mandatory constitutional responsibility for applying and administering a large portion of these laws. These arrangements are similar to those in Austria and Switzerland although the Swiss cantons have jurisdiction over a more limited range of subject matters. A significant difference in the German federation, however, is that the Länder in Germany are more directly involved in the federal government decision-making process through the representation of their first ministers and senior cabinet ministers in the federal second chamber, the Bundesrat, which possesses a veto on all federal legislation affecting the Länder. (About 60 percent of federal legislation falls into this category.) Thus the Bundesrat is a key institution in the interlocking federal-state relationship within the German federation. Within that framework, the Länder are marked by symmetry in their relative powers, although special financial arrangements have been necessary for the five new eastern Länder.

Both the federal and Land institutions are parliamentary in form. The Federal Chancellor and Cabinet are responsible to the Bundestag, but there is a formal head of state, the President of the Federal Republic, elected by an electoral college consisting of the Bundestag and an equal number of members elected by the legislatures of the Länder. The federal parliament is bicameral, with the second chamber composed of ex officio instructed delegates of the Land governments.

The German federation is of interest because of the manner in which the relationships between the federal and state governments interlock and because of the way in which the unique Bundesrat serves as a key institution in these interdependent processes.

2.2 SELECTED MULTILINGUAL FEDERATIONS IN DEVELOPING COUNTRIES

India (1950)

India became independent in 1947 and its parliament, serving also as a constituent assembly, drafted the new constitution which came into effect on 26 January 1950 establishing the Federal Union of India. Its federal features followed closely the *Government of India Act, 1935* under which the British government had attempted a federal solution to resolve the problems facing India at the time, an act which itself had been modelled on the *British North America Act, 1867*. Given the vast, populous and variegated nature of India and concerns with the threat of insecurity and disintegration, the Constituent Assembly concluded that the soundest framework was "a federation with a strong Centre." Today, the federation comprises 25 states, 7 union territories, 1 federacy and 1 associated state with a total population of over 850 million people.

India is a diverse multilingual society. Hindi, the official language, spoken by no more than 40 percent of the population (mostly in the north) and there are 18 recognized regional languages. Between 1956 and 1966 the states were reorganized largely on an ethno-linguistic basis and in one case (Punjab) on a religio-linguistic basis.

While the founders sought to create a centralized federation, the ethno-linguistic basis of many of the states and the powerful forces of regionalism within the Indian sub-continent have meant in practice a federation that is only partially centralized and has powerful states. The constitution provides for three exhaustive lists of legislative powers — exclusive federal powers, exclusive provincial powers and concurrent powers (with federal paramountcy) — and for residual powers assigned to the Union government. There is a degree of asymmetry with respect to the state of Jammu and Kashmir, which has been given powers different from those of other states. Asymmetrical relationships have also applied to some of the smaller new states established in tribal areas. Formally, the Union government possesses very substantial powers, especially powers of intervention and preemption in emergencies, but it functions within an ethno-political and multi-party context that requires that those powers be used for the most part to preserve federalism in form and spirit.

The institutions of the Union and state governments are parliamentary in form with responsible cabinet government at both levels. The head of state is a president elected by an electoral college consisting of the elected members of both houses of parliament and the state legislatures. The formal heads of the states, the governors, are appointed by the Union government.

India as a federation is of particular interest to Canadians because it has used a structure originally influenced by the Canadian model to hold together a linguistically diverse society.

Malaysia (1963)

The Malaysian federation now comprises 13 states with a population of some 19 million. It was established in 1963 when Singapore and the Borneo states of Sabah and Sarawak joined the already existing Federation of Malaya which had achieved independence in 1957. Singapore was expelled from the Federation of Malaysia just two years later, and since that time the federation has consisted of the 11 states on the Malay peninsula and the two more autonomous states on the island of Borneo.

A significant political feature of Malaysia is the diversity of its population in terms of race, ethnicity, language, religion and social customs. The population is approximately 59 percent Malay and other indigenous peoples, 32 percent Chinese and 9 percent Indian. Malays are in a majority in most of the peninsular states, but there are strong concentrations of Chinese in the west coast states, and other indigenous peoples, composed of a variety of linguistic groups, form the vast majority in the two Borneo states. The federal system has been an important factor therefore in maintaining the delicate communal balance within the federation.

As in India, the Malaysian federation is characterized by a high degree of centralization derived from the preceding Malayan constitution, itself modelled on the *Government of India Act, 1935*, and hence indirectly on the *British North America Act, 1867*. Like India, there are three exhaustive lists of powers (exclusive federal, exclusive state and concurrent) but the residual powers are assigned to the state governments. Perhaps the most distinguishing feature of the Malaysian distribution of powers is the considerable degree of asymmetry in the legislative, executive and financial autonomy ascribed to the constituent units. The 11 states of the Malay peninsula — the original states of the Federation of Malaya — stand in a symmetrical relationship to the federal government, but the two Borneo states have been allocated greater autonomy as a means of safeguarding their special "non-Malayan" interests.

Malaysia has incorporated the institutions of cabinets responsible to the legislature within both levels of government, but it has a unique form of rotating monarchy to provide the formal head of state of the federation. The *Yang di-Pertuan Agong* is selected for a five-year term from among the hereditary rulers of nine of the Malay states.

The Malaysian Federation is of interest because it is a complex delicate balance of diverse communities within a parliamentary federation and it incorporates asymmetry in the powers of constituent states in order to safeguard particular interests.

2.3 RECENTLY EMERGED AND EMERGING FEDERATIONS

Belgium (1993)

Belguim was founded in 1830 as a unitary constitutional monarchy but four stages of devolution, in 1970, 1980, 1988 and 1993, have culminated in a formal federation with a population of just over 10 million people. It is composed of six constituent units. Three are regions territorially defined (the Flemish, Walloon and Brussels Regions) with councils responsible largely for regional economic matters. Overlapping these are three Communities (the Dutch-speaking, French-speaking and German-speaking Communities) with their own councils responsible mainly for cultural and educational matters. The former represent a *territorial* jurisdiction and the latter a *personal* jurisdiction.

The main motive force for the process of devolutionary federalization has been the political polarization of the two main linguistic groups, the Dutch-speaking (58 percent) and French-speaking (41 percent) Belgians. The German-speaking minority constitutes less than one percent of the population. The bipolar character of Belgian politics has been accentuated by the greater prosperity of the Flemish region (reversing the nineteenth century situation) and by the resentment of the Dutch-speaking majority at the political dominance that had traditionally been exercised by the French-speaking Belgians within the unitary Belgian state.

The distribution of powers, because of the devolutionary character of the federalization process, has generally taken the form of specifying the increased powers of the regional and community councils leaving the unspecified residual jurisdiction with the central government. Nevertheless, in 1993 it was agreed (although yet to be implemented) that the distribution of powers should be redrafted to enumerate federal powers and leave residual jurisdiction to the constituent units. Three features distinguish the Belgian distribution of powers: the progressive devolution has in fact produced a high degree of decentralization; the powers allocated to each order of government have been mostly in the form of exclusive powers; and there has resulted a considerable measure of asymmetry among the constituent units illustrated by the difference between Regions and Communities, the differing interrelationships between Regional and Community councils in the Dutch-speaking and French-speaking areas, and the particular situation of Brussels as the capital located in the Flemish Region but with a French-speaking majority.

The federal institutions of the Belgian federation are those of a constitutional monarchy with a cabinet responsible to the Chamber of Deputies in a bicameral parliament.

Although the emergent Belgian federation is too recent to allow firm conclusions to be drawn about its operation, the devolutionary federalization process is of particular interest because of its linguistically bipolar character. It also serves as an example of a country responding to simultaneous pressures for federalization in two directions: through internal devolution, which converted it into a federation, and through external integration arising from its membership in the European Union.

Spain (1978)

Spain has also been going through a dual process of federalization relating to internal devolution and external integration within the European Union. In 1978, after some forty years of totalitarian centralization under the dictatorship of General Franco, Spain adopted a new constitution establishing a system of parliamentary democracy. As part of post-Franco democratization and as a means of balancing powerful regional interests fostered by revived Basque and Catalonian nationalism, Spain has pursued a process of regionalization. It has provided for units called "Autonomous Communities" of which there are 17 in a country of nearly 40 million.

Although traditionally a strongly centralized unitary state, Spain has in fact contained considerable diversity. While the political culture of the Castilians has tended to be hierarchical and centralistic, the Aragonese, Basques, Catalonians, Galicians, Navarrese and Valencians have each had a strong interest in preserving their way of life and securing the power to maintain their cultural identity.

The Spanish response to this situation after the adoption of the 1978 constitution was to grant each region its own state of autonomy tailored to its particular situation or based upon a particular set of compromises negotiated between the regional leadership and the central government. Subsequent actions of the Madrid government have, however, held to a more uniform distribution of jurisdiction. Although the different regions are proceeding to autonomy at different speeds, the intention is that ultimately the situation of the autonomous communities will be less asymmetrical. While the Spanish constitution does not define itself as explicitly federal, it does provide for lists of powers that are exclusive to either the general or regional governments, while leaving the residual power to the central government. Thus, Spain is a federation in all but name with the 17 autonomous communities possessing constitutional authority for a considerable degree of self-rule.

The central government is a parliamentary monarchy with the Council of Ministers responsible to the lower house of the Cortes, Spain's bicameral legislature. The Senate, the second chamber of the Cortes, serves as a representative body for the regions of Spain.

As a unitary state engaged in devolutionary federalization within its own borders by a process characterized by considerable asymmetry Spain is an interesting example of an effort to accommodate variations in the strengths of regional pressures for autonomy.

2.4 BICOMMUNAL FEDERATIONS THAT HAVE SEPARATED

Czechoslovakia (1920-1992)

Prior to its split at the end of 1992, Czechoslovakia (the Czech and Slovak Federative Republic) was a two-unit federation of the Czech and Slovak Republics. This bicommunal federation was designed to provide its two primary constituent communities with a measure of self-government while maintaining a strong federation to manage the differences between the two communities.

Czechoslovakia was established after World War I in the wake of the breakup of the Austro-Hungarian empire. Initially it was a unitary democratic republic uniting the Czechs and Slovaks. This allowed the Czechs to have more autonomy from the Austrians and Germans, and the Slovaks to escape from Hungarian domination. The Slovaks, who comprised one-third of the population, chafed under Czech domination and the limited autonomy devolved to them. This attitude manifested itself under the arrangements that existed during the German occupation and the post-war Communist regime. During the 1968 liberalization led by Alexander Dubcek the establishment of a federal constitution to accommodate the separate ethnic interests of the Czechs and Slovaks was promised. The resulting Soviet military intervention brought an end to the liberalizing reforms, but the commitment to ethnic accommodation was retained and a formally federal constitution took effect. Over the next two decades the country was effectively centralized both economically and politically under the control of the Communist Party. Within this regime Slovakia experienced rapid economic growth and Slovak opportunities to enter both their national and the federal bureaucracy were expanded, but the federal character of the constitution had little more than nominal significance. Following the collapse of the Communist regime in 1989, the nominally federal system remained intact with a bicameral Federal Assembly and unicameral National Councils in Slovakia and the Czech Republic. The federation encompassed a population of nearly 16 million people.

In the period that followed, however, the Slovak nationalists sought a confederation of the two states in which Slovakia would control its own economy and foreign policy. The Czechs, however, saw little advantage in maintaining their links with Slovakia unless they continued to be part of a full federation. In 1992 the Slovak Nationalist party gained power in Slovakia and demanded independence. Subsequently, a Slovak-led coalition blocked the re-election of President Vaclav Hável. This precipitated an agreement between the Czech and Slovak leaders, each of whom saw political advantages in to proceeding without the other group, on a plan for the peaceful division of Czechoslovakia into two independent states by 1 January 1993. Without any referendums or further elections to ascertain the views of the electorate, the country was divided on that date.

Czechoslovakia during the 1989-92 post-Communist period existed in a different international climate from Canada and its disintegration was less the secession of one unit from a larger federation than the separation of two entities. Nonetheless the case deserves close attention.[9] It illustrates the particular problems and tensions that can arise in a bicommunal federation from the dynamic process of cumulative bipolarization, and the speed with which disintegration can occur when political leaders on each side see disengagement as mutually profitable to their own political positions.

Pakistan (1947-1971)

Following the partition of India in 1947, Pakistan, with a total population of about 90 million, was a country of two large fragments severed from the structure of old India, each of these parts different in every way except one — religion — and separated by a thousand miles of hostile territory. The result was a federation of

two basic units, West Pakistan, largely Urdu-speaking, Middle-Eastern in character, and the wealthier unit, and East Pakistan, Bengali-speaking, South-East Asian
in outlook, and the more populous with 55 percent of the population. Between
1947 and 1956 the *Government of India Act, 1935*, served as a working interim
federal constitution for Pakistan. During this period Pakistan consisted of one
province in the east and three provinces and a variety of other units in the west.
Finally, in 1956 the new constitution came into force establishing a federation
composed of two provinces (the various previous units in the west being amalga-
mated into a single unitary province). The two provinces were given parity of
representation in a unicameral federal legislature.

The adoption of the new constitution did not decrease of the political polarization between East and West Pakistan that had characterized government under the
interim constitution. In 1958, Pakistan's first military regime took power and issued
its own constitution reaffirming the two-unit federation. The Bengalis, chafing at
the dominance of the western province in their political and economic life, and
feeling that they had been treated as a colony by the government in Rawalpindi,
declared the secession in 1971 of East Pakistan, or Bangladesh as they renamed
it. This resulted in two weeks of civil war and the birth of the independent state of
Bangladesh. For its part the former "unitary" single province of West Pakistan
under a new constitution in 1973 itself became a federation of four provinces.

The bipolar tensions within Pakistan that led to the civil war and the division of
the country illustrate the difficulties and instability that have characterized two-
unit federations.

Chapter 3

The Distribution of Powers in Federations

3.1 THE ISSUE OF BALANCING UNITY AND DIVERSITY

In all the federations described in the preceding section, a common feature has been the existence at one and the same time of powerful motives to be united for certain purposes and of deep-rooted motives for autonomous regional governments for other purposes. This has expressed itself in the design of these federations by the distribution of powers between those assigned to the federal government for the purposes shared in common and those assigned to the regional units of government for the purposes related to the expression of regional identity. Thus the defining institutional characteristic of these federations has been the combination within a single political system of shared-rule and self-rule through the constitutional distribution of powers between the federal and regional governments.

The specific form and allocation of the distribution of powers has varied relating to the underlying degrees and kinds of common interests and diversity within the particular society in question. Different geographical, historical, economic, ecological, security, linguistic, cultural, intellectual, demographic and international factors and the interrelation of these have been significant in contributing to the strength of the motives for union and for regional identity, and therefore have affected the particular distribution of powers in different federations. Generally the more the degree of homogeneity within a society the greater the powers that have been allocated to the federal government, and the more the degree of diversity the greater the powers that have been assigned to the constituent units of government. Even in the latter case it has often been considered desirable, however, that the federal government should have sufficient powers to resist tendencies to balkanization.

In addition to expressing a balance between unity and diversity, the design of federations has also required a balance between the independence and interdependence of the federal and regional governments in relation to each other. The classic view of federation, which tended to prevail when the Canadian federation was established, considered the ideal distribution of powers between governments in a federation to be one in which each government was able to act independently within its own watertight sphere of responsibility.[10] In practice federations have found it impossible to avoid overlaps in the responsibilities of government and a measure of interdependence is typical of all federations. An example of this in its most extreme form is the interlocking relationship between governments in the German federation which has developed because some 60 percent of federal legislation is administered by the states. Such a strong emphasis upon coordination through joint decision making may carry its own price in terms of reduction in opportunities for flexibility and variety of policy through autonomous decision making by different governments. There is therefore a need to find a balance between the independence and interdependence of governments within a federation.

The process by which federations are established may affect the character of the distribution of powers. Where the process of establishment has involved the aggregation of previously distinct units giving up some of their sovereignty to establish a new federal government, the emphasis has usually been upon specifying a limited set of exclusive and concurrent federal powers with the residual (usually unspecified) powers remaining with the constituent units. The United States, Switzerland and Australia provide classic examples. Austria and Germany followed this traditional pattern although their reconstruction during the post-war period did involve some devolutionary elements. Where the creation of a federation has involved a process of devolution from a formerly unitary state, the reverse has usually been the case: the powers of regional units have been specified and the residual authority has remained with the federal government. Belgium and Spain provide examples. Some federations like Canada, India and Malaysia have involved a combination of these processes of aggregation and devolution, and they have listed specifically exclusive federal, exclusive provincial, and concurrent powers with the residual authority, in Canada and India (and the earlier Malayan Federation) but not in the Malaysian Federation, assigned to the federal government.

3.2 RELATIONSHIP BETWEEN DISTRIBUTIONS OF LEGISLATIVE AND EXECUTIVE POWERS

In some federations, particularly those in the Anglo-Saxon tradition, each order of government has generally been assigned executive responsibilities in the same fields for which it has legislative powers. Classical examples are the USA, Canada and Australia. There are several reasons for favouring such an arrangement. First, it reinforces the autonomy of the legislative bodies. Second, it assures to each government the authority to implement its own legislation which might otherwise prove meaningless. Third, where the principle of parliamentary executives responsible to their legislatures has been adopted, it is only if legislative and executive jurisdiction coincide that the legislature can exercise control over the body executing its laws.

In European federations, particularly Switzerland, Austria and Germany, more commonly administrative responsibility has not coincided with legislative authority, administration for many areas of federal legislative authority being assigned by the constitution to the governments of the constituent units. This enables the federal legislature to lay down considerable uniform legislation while leaving this to be applied by regional governments in ways that take account of varying regional circumstances. Such an arrangement does in practice require more extensive collaboration between the levels of government, however.

In practice the contrast between these two approaches is not quite so sharp. Even in the Anglo-Saxon federations federal governments have delegated considerable responsibilities for federal programs to constituent governments often by providing financial assistance through grant-in-aid programs. Furthermore, in Canada the constitution itself provides an exception to the general pattern by providing for federal legislation and provincial administration in the sphere of criminal law. Newer federations in former British colonial areas such as India and Malaysia have also provided in their constitutions for state administration of federal laws made in areas of shared concurrent jurisdiction. On the other hand, Belgium contrasts with the other European federations, since the allocation of executive powers is closely tied to the allocation of legislative powers. The current Russian constitution on the other hand stipulates that the federal and unit executive bodies constitute a single system of executive authority within the federation.

3.3 VARIATIONS IN THE FORM OF THE DISTRIBUTION OF LEGISLATIVE AUTHORITY

Exclusive Legislative Powers

In Switzerland, Canada and more recently Belgium, most legislative powers are assigned exclusively to either the federal or constituent unit governments. By contrast, in the United States and Australia the powers assigned exclusively to the federal government are very much more limited with most federal powers being identified as shared concurrent powers. In Austria, Germany, India and Malaysia there are fairly extensive categories of both exclusive and shared concurrent powers constitutionally specified.

The advantage of assigning a responsibility exclusively to one government or another is two-fold. It reinforces the autonomy of that government and it makes clear which government is accountable for policy in that area. In practice, however, even where most powers have been assigned exclusively to one level of government or the other, experience, such as that of Switzerland and Canada, has indicated that overlaps of jurisdiction are unavoidable because it is virtually impossible to define watertight compartments of exclusive jurisdiction.

Concurrent (Shared) Legislative Powers

The recognition of the inevitability of overlaps and the need for shared jurisdiction and collaboration in many areas has led to extensive areas of concurrent legislative jurisdiction being allocated in the constitutions of the U.S.A., Australia, Germany, India and Malaysia. By contrast in Canada the only constitutionally specified areas of concurrent jurisdiction are agriculture, immigration, old age pensions and benefits, and export of nonrenewable natural resources, forest products and electrical energy.

Concurrency has a number of advantages in federations. It has provided an element of flexibility in the distribution of powers, enabling the federal government to postpone the exercise of potential authority in a particular field until it becomes a matter of federal importance. The constituent governments can thus be left in the meantime to pursue their own initiatives. The federal government may use concurrent jurisdiction to legislate federation-wide standards while giving regional governments room to legislate the details and to deliver the services in a manner sensitive to local circumstances. Indeed, in Austria and Germany there is a special constitutional category of concurrent jurisdiction specifying a federal power to enact "framework legislation" only and leaving the Länder to fill out that area with more detailed law. Concurrent lists of legislative power also avoid the necessity of enumerating complicated minute subdivisions of individual functions to be assigned exclusively to one area of government or the other, and reduce the likelihood that such minute subdivisions will over time become obsolete in changing circumstances.

Normally where concurrent jurisdiction is specified, the constitution has specified that in cases of conflict between federal law and unit law the federal law prevails. One notable exception occurs in Canada where old age pensions are an area of concurrent jurisdiction but in cases of conflict provincial law prevails over federal law. This has enabled Quebec to preserve its own pension system and other provinces to accept federal pension jurisdiction.

Residual Powers

The residual power represents assignment by the constitution of jurisdiction over those matters not otherwise listed in the constitution. In most federations, especially those created by a process of aggregating previously separate units, the residual power has been assigned to the unit governments. Examples are the U.S.A.,

Switzerland, Australia, Austria, Germany, Malaysia and Czechoslovakia. In some federations, however, usually where devolution from a more centralized unitary regime characterized the process of federal formation, the residual powers were left with the federal government. Examples have been Canada, India, the Federation of Malaya before it was expanded into Malaysia, and Belgium, although in the case of Belgium it has been agreed (but yet to be implemented) to reformulate the constitutional distribution of powers so that the residual power lies with the unit governments.

The significance of the residual powers is related to the number and comprehensiveness of the enumerated lists of legislative power. The greater the enumeration of powers the less significant the residual power. Thus in federations like India and Malaysia and to a lesser extent Canada where the constitutions set out three exhaustive and comprehensive lists of exclusive federal, exclusive provincial and concurrent legislative powers, the residual power has been relatively less significant than in federations like the U.S.A., Australia and Germany where the state powers were not enumerated but simply covered by a substantial unspecified residual power. In these latter federations the assignment of a significant residual power to the states was intended to underline their autonomy and the limited nature of powers assigned to the federal government. It is important to note, however, that in practice there has been a tendency in these federations for the courts to read the maximum "implied powers" into the specified federal authority at the expense of the scope of the residual state powers, thus producing a tendency over time towards the progressive centralization of government powers. Paradoxically, in such federations as Canada, India and Malaysia where the centralist founders enumerated what were intended to be limited specific provincial powers, there has been a tendency for the courts to read those powers broadly thus tempering the expansion of federal authority.

In a few federations the constitution provides the federal government with specific override or emergency powers to invade or curtail in certain conditions otherwise normally provincial constitutional powers. These have been the result of the fears of their founders about the prospects of potential balkanization or disintegration. The most extensive examples of such quasi-unitary powers are found in the Indian and Malaysian constitutions, but the Canadian constitution also includes some such powers (e.g. the reservation and disallowance powers; the declaratory power; and the peace, order and good government clause as interpreted by the courts).

3.4 THE SCOPE OF LEGISLATIVE POWERS ALLOCATED

Apart from the form that the constitutional distribution of powers has taken, the particular powers assigned to each order of government has also varied from federation to federation according to the particular circumstances and balance of interests within each federation. For a detailed comparative tabulation of the distribution of powers in the different federations compared in this study see Appendix A.

Generally speaking, in most federations international relations, defence, the functioning of the economic and monetary union, major taxing powers and interregional transportation have been assigned to the jurisdiction of the federal government. Social affairs (including education, health services, social welfare and labour services), maintenance of law and security, and local government have usually been assigned to the regional governments, although parts of these areas, especially relating to social services are often shared as is the area of agriculture and natural resources. Nevertheless, as is clear from Appendix A, there is considerable variation in the specific allocations within different federations.

Some subject matters have proved particularly troublesome. One of these is that of foreign affairs where, in many federations, federal jurisdiction may be used to override jurisdiction that would otherwise belong to the regional governments. In a few federations, however, the federal treaty power has been limited by the requirement that where treaties affect the jurisdiction of regional governments consultation must occur or their consent must be obtained. In the case of Canada, implementing provincial legislation is required where applicable. Coordinating public debt has also sometimes been a problem because a constituent unit government may by its borrowing affect the credit-worthiness of other governments within the federation. This led in Australia to provision for the coordination of public borrowing by an intergovernmental Loans Council with power to make decisions binding on both levels of government. In some other federations such concerns have led to federal control of public borrowing, particularly foreign borrowing, by constituent unit governments.

Two areas where in practice there has tended to be extensive activity by both levels of government have been economic policy and social affairs. In the former, regional units of government have been concerned to ensure the economic welfare of their own citizens and to develop policies related to their own particular economic interests. This has sometimes extended to the establishing of trade offices in foreign countries to encourage both trade and investment, a pattern not unique to Canada being found in other federations such as the United States, Australia and Germany. In the area of social affairs, including health, education and social services, regional governments have usually had primary constitutional responsibility. But, commonly, extensive federal financial assistance has often been necessary because of program costs and because of the pressures for federation-wide standards of service to citizens.

3.5 DISTRIBUTION OF ADMINISTRATIVE RESPONSIBILITIES

As already noted in section 3.2, in a number of federations, especially those in the Anglo-Saxon tradition, e.g. the U.S.A., Canada and Australia, the distribution of administrative responsibilities in most matters corresponds with the distribution of legislative authority. However, in some federations, there are constitutionally mandated and entrenched provisions for splitting legislative and administrative jurisdiction in an area between different orders of government. These permanent and constitutionalized arrangements are to be distinguished from temporary delegations of legislative and executive authority that also occur in many federations. Examples of extensive constitutionalized allocation of executive and administrative responsibilities differing from the allocation of legislative jurisdiction occur in Switzerland, Austria, Germany, India and Malaysia. In all five, autonomous canton and state governments are constitutionally responsible for the implementation and administration of a wide range of federal legislation. In Germany, India and Malaysia all federal legislation enacted in the area of concurrent jurisdiction is specified by the constitution as resting with the states for its administration. Thus, while these federations are relatively centralized legislatively, they are much more decentralized administratively. These federations have shown that benefits can flow from the administrative decentralization of federal legislation particularly in adapting it to the different circumstances and sensitivities of the various regions.

Chapter 4

The Distribution of Finances

4.1 IMPORTANCE OF THE ALLOCATION OF FINANCIAL RESOURCES

The allocation of financial resources to each order of government within a federation is important for two main reasons: first, these resources enable or constrain governments in the exercise of their constitutionally assigned legislative and executive responsibilities; second, taxing powers and expenditure are themselves important instruments for affecting and regulating the economy.

4.2 THE DISTRIBUTION OF REVENUE POWERS

Most federations specify in their constitutions (or in the case of Belgium in special legislation) the revenue-raising powers of the two orders of government. For a comparative tabulation of these see the appropriate section of Appendix A. The major taxing powers usually identified are customs and excise, corporate taxes, personal income taxes and various sales and consumption taxes. Customs and excise taxes have almost always been placed under federal jurisdiction in the interests of ensuring an effective internal customs and economic union. Corporate income taxes have also most often come under federal jurisdiction because corporations in earning their income tend to cross the boundaries of the internal regional units and the location of their headquarters does not necessarily reflect the geographical sources of their income. Nevertheless, in some federations this taxation may be shared and if so usually under concurrent jurisdiction. Personal income taxes may be more directly attributed to location of residence and therefore is often an area shared by federal and regional governments although in some federations it has been exclusively federal (e.g. Austria, India and Czechoslovakia).

Sales and consumption taxes are areas which in most federations both federal and regional governments share although there are some exceptions to this pattern.

A common characteristic of the allocation of fiscal powers in nearly all federations is that the majority of major revenue sources have been assigned to the federal governments. Even where some tax fields are shared or placed under concurrent jurisdiction, the federal governments tend to predominate because of the federal power to preempt a field of concurrent jurisdiction and because of provisions limiting the range of tax sources, both direct and indirect, that regional governments have been assigned. Two factors have been particularly influential in creating this general pattern. One is the concentration of resources in the federal government necessary if it is to perform the redistributive role usually expected of it. The other is the influence of Keynesian theories concerning policies for economic stability and development prevalent at the time that many of the current federal fiscal arrangements were developed in these federations.

In addition to taxation there are two other important sources for governmental raising of funds. The first is public borrowing, a source open to both levels of government in most federations although foreign borrowing in some cases (most notably Austria, India and Malaysia) is placed under exclusive federal jurisdiction. In the case of Australia all major public borrowing by both levels is coordinated through the operation of the intergovernmental Loans Council. The second source is the operation of public corporations and enterprises, the profits of which may serve as a source of governmental income. In most federations this latter is a source open to both levels of government.

4.3 THE ALLOCATION OF EXPENDITURE POWERS

Broadly speaking the distribution of expenditure powers in each federation corresponds to the combined scope of the legislative and administrative responsibilities assigned to each government within the federation. But several points should be noted.

First, where the administration of a substantial portion of federal legislation is constitutionally assigned to the governments of the constituent units as in Switzerland, Austria, Germany, India and Malaysia, the constitutional expenditure responsibilities of the regional governments are significantly broader than would be indicated by the distribution of legislative powers taken alone.

Second, the expenditure requirements of different areas of responsibilities may vary. For instance, in relative terms health, education and social services are higher cost functions by comparison with functions relating more to regulation than the provision of services.

Third, in most federations the spending power of each order of government has not been limited strictly to the enumerated legislative and administrative jurisdiction. Governments have usually been taken to possess a *general* spending power.

Thus, federal governments have used their general spending power to pursue certain objectives in areas of state jurisdiction by providing grants to regional governments that otherwise could not afford to provide the services being demanded of them. For their part constituent unit governments have in a number of federations, including Canada, used their general spending power to establish trade and promotion offices outside the federation even where there was no constitutional jurisdiction in external affairs specified.

The use of the federal spending power in areas of exclusive provincial jurisdiction has been politically contentious in Canadian intergovernmental relations but has not been successfully challenged in the courts. The practice is not unique to the Canadian federation, however. It has occurred extensively in the U.S.A. and Australia since the economic depression of the 1930s. Regional governments in federations have frequently accepted the federal assistance but where it has taken the form of grants with conditions attached they have resented this as an invasion of their areas of exclusive jurisdiction. This has particularly been the case where federal spending on matters within regional authority is commenced uninvited or is withdrawn without notice. In both Canada and the United States such unilateral withdrawals of assistance have led to charges of "off loading" and of "fend-for-yourself federalism."

It should be noted that in such older federations as the United States, Canada and Australia where the use of the federal general spending power has been widespread, the constitution does not explicitly identify a general spending power. Nonetheless, their courts in varying degrees have recognized that the taxing and appropriating powers of the federal government can be used to affect a field of activity beyond the strict confines of its normal legislative powers. The newer federal constitutions of India and Malaysia, designed in the light of practice in the older federations, have made explicit recognition in their constitutions of the authority of their federal governments to provide grants to state governments for *any* purpose, whether that purpose is under federal government jurisdiction or not.

In those federations where the constitution assigns to the state governments administrative responsibility for a considerable portion of federal legislation, substantial federal transfers, either as portions of federal tax proceeds or in the form of unconditional and conditional grants, are a typical feature.

4.4 THE ISSUE OF VERTICAL AND HORIZONTAL IMBALANCES

Virtually every federation has found the need to correct two kinds of financial imbalances. The vertical imbalances occur when constitutionally assigned federal and unit government revenues do not match their constitutionally assigned expenditure responsibilities. These imbalances occur generally for two reasons. First, it has usually been found desirable to allocate the major taxing powers to the federal government because these are closely related to the development of the customs union and more broadly to an effective economic union, while some of the most expensive expenditure responsibilities such as health, education and social services have usually been considered best administered on a regional basis where particular regional circumstances can be taken into account. Tables 7 and 8 read together illustrate the differences in the proportions of total (federal-state-local combined) revenues and of total (federal-state-local combined) expenditure responsibilities of federal governments in the different federations. A second reason for vertical imbalances is that no matter how carefully the original designers of the federation may attempt to match the revenue resources and expenditure responsibilities of each order of government, over time the significance of different taxes changes (such as income taxes and consumption taxes) and the costs of expenditures vary in unforeseen ways. Consequently, there is a need to build in processes whereby these imbalances can be adjusted from time to time.

Horizontal imbalances represent a second form that require correction. Horizontal imbalances occur when the revenue capacities of different constituent units vary so that they are not able to provide their citizens with services at the same level on the basis of comparable tax levels. In addition to horizontal revenue imbalances, there can also be interprovincial imbalances on the expenditure side due to differences in the "expenditure needs" of different constituent units because of variations in sociodemographic characteristics of their populations such as population dispersion, urbanization, social composition and age structure, and the cost of providing services affected by such factors as the scale of public administration and the physical and economic environment.

TABLE 7:   Federal Government Revenues Before Intergovernmental Transfers as a Percentage of Total (Federal-State-Local) Government Revenues

	1981	*1991*
Malaysia	86.4	90.0
Austria	73.8	72.9
Australia	76.2	71.3
India	66.8	67.6
Germany	64.3	66.1
United States	65.3	56.5
Canada	49.4	48.2
Switzerland	32.0	36.5

Sources: *Government Financial Statistics Yearbooks,* Advisory Commission on Intergovernmental Relations (Washington), *Significant Features of Fiscal Federalism,* 1984 edition, p. 10, 1993 edition, p. 12, and *Annuaire statistique de la Suisse.*

TABLE 8: Federal Government Expenditures After Intergovernmental Transfers as a Percentage of Total (Federal-State-Local) Government Expenditures

	1981	*1991*
Malaysia	82.9	82.2
Austria	68.8	69.3
Germany	58.7	62.4
United States	61.3	53.8
Australia	52.8	50.9
India	42.2	45.1
Canada	40.3	40.8
Switzerland	23.3	27.4

Sources: *Government Financial Statistics Yearbooks,* Advisory Commission on Intergovernmental Relations (Washington), *Significant Features of Fiscal Federalism,* 1984 edition, p. 12, 1993 edition, volume 2, p. 12, and *Annuaire statistique de la Suisse.*

4.5 THE ROLE OF FINANCIAL TRANSFERS

In order to correct these imbalances most federations have arrangements for financial transfers from one level of government to another. Because federal governments generally have controlled the major tax sources, transfers have usually taken the form of transfers to the regional units of government. Their purpose has been both to remove vertical imbalances by transfers in the form of tax-shares, unconditional block grants or specific-purpose conditional grants, and to remove horizontal imbalances to assist poorer units. Table 9 gives an indication of the significance of these transfers as a portion of total provincial or state revenues and the degree of resulting provincial or state dependence on transfers.

TABLE 9:   Intergovernmental Transfers as a Percentage of Provincial or
State Revenue

	1981	*1991*
Australia	50.6	45.4
India	41.8	43.0
Austria	43.3	41.2
Malaysia	20.4	25.2
Switzerland	25.9	21.7*
United States	25.1	21.4
Canada	20.4	18.3
Germany	18.1	16.7

*This data is for 1990.

Sources: *Government Financial Statistics Yearbooks* and *Annuaire statistique de la Suisse* and Bernard Dafflon, *Fédéralisme et solidarité - Étude de la péréquation financiére en Suisse,* PIFF Etudes et colloques No15, Fribourg 1995.

4.6 CONDITIONAL OR UNCONDITIONAL TRANSFERS

The degree of provincial or state dependence is affected not only by the proportion that federal transfers represent in their revenues but also by whether these transfers are conditional or unconditional in character. Federal transfers to regional units of government may have conditions attached to them in order to influence how they are spent. This "golden lead," as it is referred to in Germany, may however undermine the autonomy of the regional units of government especially if conditional transfers constitute a high proportion of the transfers and hence a significant portion of total state or provincial revenues. To avoid this, transfers may take the form of unconditional transfers (either set percentages of certain federal tax proceeds as occurs in many of the newer federations or unconditional block grants). Although strictly comparable statistics are difficult to obtain, there is clearly a considerable variation among federations in the extent to which federal transfers have been conditional or unconditional. Data obtained from various sources in the individual federations indicates that the proportion of conditional transfers appears to have been highest in the United States (over 80 percent) and Malaysia (68 percent) ranging down to Australia (34 percent) with most of the other federations somewhere between. The figure for Canada depends on whether the Established Program Financing (EPF) transfers, now converted into the Canadian Health and Social Transfer (CHST) system which are at most semi-conditional in character are regarded as conditional or unconditional. If these transfers are classified as conditional the comparable Canadian figure for the proportion of transfers that are conditional would be 63.34 percent for 1991, but if they are classified as unconditional the proportion would be 25.56 percent.

The proportion of total state or provincial revenue made up by federal conditional transfers provides one significant measure of the constraints upon state or provincial autonomy. In most federations conditional transfers constitute between 10 and 20 percent of total state or provincial revenues. In Canada, if the EPF transfers are classified as conditional, the figure for 1991 would be 11.86 percent but if they are classified as unconditional it would be 3.99 percent (lowest among all federations).[11]

Arguments have been advanced in support of both forms of transfer. In support of conditional grants has been an argument which has particularly tended to dominate discussion of the subject in the United States. This is based on the principle of financial responsibility and accountability, i.e. that the federal government that has the nasty task of raising the funds by taxation should, in the interests of accountability to the tax-payer, control and set the conditions for the use of these funds by the state governments. Consequently, in recent decades, conditional grants have always represented at least 80 percent of the federal transfers in the United States.

Countering this, however, is the concern to which more attention has been paid in some other federations that conditional grants are likely to undermine the autonomy of the regional units of government by inducing them to undertake expenditures not necessarily in tune with their own priorities. Furthermore, in those federations where the regional units of government have parliamentary executives responsible to their own legislatures, it has been argued that these governments can be held responsible for the use of unconditional transfers through their accountability to their own legislatures and hence electorates. These arguments have led in the case of most parliamentary federations to a significantly lower reliance upon conditional transfers and a higher proportion of unconditional transfers than in the United States

4.7 EQUALIZATION TRANSFERS

The importance of "equalization" transfers lies in the view that all citizens within a federation should be entitled to comparable services without having to be subject to excessively different tax rates. The need for such transfers has arisen in most federations from a recognition that disparities in wealth among regions within a federation are likely to have a corrosive effect on cohesion within a federation. Indeed, it is for this reason that in most European federations equalization transfers have been labelled "solidarity" transfers.

The arrangements for equalization transfers have varied from federation to federation and these are set out in summary form in Table 10. Several points are especially noteworthy. First, the extent of the equalization transfers varies

TABLE 10: Equalization Arrangements

United States	no generalized equalization scheme: some equalization occurs from cumulative effect of provisions in specific federal grant-in-aid schemes as approved by Congress.
Switzerland	federal transfers: based on formulae involving a range of criteria ranking cantons by financial capacity as the basis for tax-sharing and conditional grants, but the equalizing transfer system is smaller than in Germany, Canada and Australia.
Canada	federal transfers: equalization scheme based on formula (adjusted from time to time) averaging representative set of provincial taxes and providing unconditional grants representing 42% of all transfers.
Australia	federal transfers: based between 1933 and 1981-82 on recommendations derived from determination of needs of claimant states by a standing independent Commonwealth Grants Commission; since 1981-82 has taken form of adjustments to the general Adjustment Grant transfers based on calculation of relativities of expenditure needs among states.
Germany	primarily inter-state transfers (62%): equalization through an inter-state revenue pool to which rich Länder pay and from which poor Länder draw according to a formula; plus federal transfers (38%): Federal Supplementary Payments of 1.5% of value-added tax (VAT). The primary per capita distribution of the shares of the Länder of a portion of the VAT also has an equalizing effect.
Austria	federal transfers: Länder receive a per capita federal grant sufficient to bring their average per capita tax revenue up to the national average (a little more than half the Länder qualify). The primary distribution of provincial shares of federal taxes also has an equalization effect.
India	federal transfers: based on non-binding recommendations of quinquennial independent Finance Commissions recommending share of federal taxes and distribution of unconditional and conditional grants to fill gaps in state revenues.
Malaysia	federal transfers: determined by federal government following consultation with intergovernmental National Finance Council and based on a combination of unconditional shares of certain federal taxes and unconditional and conditional per capita grants.
Belgium	federal transfers: a "national solidarity" unconditional grant is paid to Regions where the personal income tax revenue per capita is below the national average (to adjust for the receipt by Regions of a percentage of personal income taxes on the basis of derivation).
Spain	federal transfers: since 1987 criteria including population, size, personal income, fiscal effort, number of internal provinces within Autonomous Community, and distance to state capital; applied by federal government to shares of federal tax revenue transferred to Autonomous Communities.

considerably. Most federations, with the exception of the United States, have some formal equalization scheme but the scope of such transfers has been greater in some such as Germany, Canada and Australia than in others such as Switzerland.

Second, in all but the German case, equalization is achieved by redistribution among the regional units of government effected by federal transfers to the regional units of government. Germany is unique in providing constitutionally for inter-state transfers to cover a substantial portion for adjusting horizontal imbalances. Initially this was the sole method of equalization employed in that federation, but later, federal transfers in the form of supplementary per capita payments derived from the Value Added Tax (VAT) have provided a substantial further equalizing redistribution.

Third, in Canada the effort to correct horizontal imbalances through federal equalization payments has focused primarily on adjusting for differences in the revenue capacities of the provinces. While this approach is typical of many federations, in some and most notably in Australia, there has been considerable effort to account as well for equalizing expenditure imbalances.[12]

Fourth, the form of equalization transfers to regional units of government varies. There are those that are based on an agreed formula, e.g. Switzerland, Canada, Germany, Austria, Malaysia, Belgium and Spain (although in some of these cases the federal government dominates the process of arriving at an agreement). In others, notably Australia and India, the allocations have been based largely on the recommendation of standing or periodic independent commissions (which may themselves use a variety of formulae to arrive at their recommendations).

Fifth, in some circumstances there may be a relationship between the degree of decentralization in a federation and the need for equalization arrangements. The more fiscally decentralized a federation is and the greater the inter-state disparities in revenue capacity and expenditure need, the greater is likely to be the need for equalizing mechanisms to promote horizontal balance.

Sixth, it would appear the different federations vary in terms of the tolerance of their citizens for horizontal imbalances. For example, egalitarian Australia, which is blessed with relatively modest inter-state disparities in revenue capacity, goes to great lengths to fully equalize on both the revenue and expenditure aspects. Germany also provides nearly full equalization, at least on the revenue side. The United States, with relatively large inter-state disparities but no formal equalization system at all, appears to have a much greater tolerance for horizontal imbalances. Canada lies somewhere between these two extremes. It has a substantial equalization program that, because of the particularly large revenue capacity disparities among the provinces, only delivers partial equalization. One factor affecting variations in the tolerance for horizontal imbalances in different federations is the relative value placed upon equity as opposed to provincial autonomy and non-centralization.

4.8 PROCESSES AND INSTITUTIONS FOR ADJUSTING FINANCIAL ARRANGEMENTS

Because, as already noted, the values of revenue resources and expenditure responsibilities change over time, federations have found it necessary to establish processes and institutions to facilitate dealing with vertical and horizontal imbalances. Table 11 summarizes the arenas in which these issues have been fought out in different federations. It is noteworthy that in those federations characterized by a separation of executive and legislative powers within each order of government, e.g. the United States and Switzerland, the primary arena is the federal legislature (in the Swiss case advised from time to time by ad hoc commissions). In the other federations characterized by fused parliamentary executives, the primary arena has been that of executive federalism, i.e. negotiations between the executives representing the federal and regional units of government.

In terms of the processes for adjusting issues of federal finance four distinct patterns can be identified.[13] In Australia and India, although in different form, expert commissions established by the federal government have been entrusted with the primary task of determining distributive formulae. That in Australia is a standing commission while that in India is quinquennial and established by constitutional requirement. These commissions hear representations from the state governments and report to the federal government which normally follows their recommendations. A second pattern is the constitutional provision for an intergovernmental council composed of federal and state representatives, the Malaysian National Finance Council being an example. A third pattern is exemplified by Germany, Austria, Switzerland, Belgium and the United States where grants to the states are determined by the federal government, but there are formal state representatives in the federal legislature who are involved in approving them so that state representatives are represented in the approval process (although arrangements vary in these federations). A fourth pattern is that found in Canada where the determination of equalization formula, other tax transfer programs and tax agreements are under the control of the federal government whose legislature contains no provision for formal representation of regional governments. Nevertheless, because of the importance of these issues, federal-provincial financial relations have been a matter for extended discussion in innumerable committees of federal and provincial officials and the source of much public polemics between federal and provincial governments.[14]

In virtually all federations, but most notably Australia, India, Malaysia, Germany and Canada, a variety of intergovernmental councils, commissions and committees have been developed to facilitate adaptation of the financial arrangements. Australia has gone furthest in developing such institutions with three intergovernmental institutions worth noting here. The Premiers Council plays a key role in deliberations on the transfers but is not a body established by the constitution. The Loans Council, which coordinates federal and state borrowing,

TABLE 11: Arenas for Resolving Issues of Federal Finance

United States	Congress: negotiations among representatives of different states in Congress over allocation of grant-in-aid programs.
Switzerland	Federal Parliament: negotiations within Federal Council (i.e. federal executive) and Parliament (containing cantonal representatives) assisted from time to time by commissions.
Canada	executive federalism: conferences of finance ministers and first ministers' conferences, but ultimate decision lies with Government of Canada.
Australia	executive federalism: in Premiers' Conference and in Loans Council. Ultimate decisions lie with federal government, but on transfers recommendations of independent expert Commonwealth Grants Commission are usually implemented.
Germany	executive federalism: ultimately fiscal arrangements require endorsement of Bundesrat composed of representatives of governments of Länder.
Austria	executive federalism: intergovernmental negotiation with dominant federal government role, but federal second chamber is composed of representatives of state legislatures.
India	executive federalism: intergovernmental negotiations tempered by recommendations of constitutionally required independent quinquennial Finance Commissions.
Malaysia	executive federalism: dominant role of federal government but constitutionally required to consult National Finance Council which includes a representative of each state.
Belgium	inter-party coalition bargaining within the federal government and intergovernmental negotiation.
Spain	executive federalism: negotiations between federal government and governments of Autonomous Communities (but leverage of latter is asymmetrical) but ultimately dependent on federal government decision.

was established by a constitutional amendment in 1927 and can make decisions binding both levels of government. The Commonwealth Grants Commission is a standing body that, since 1933, has advised the Australian federal government on equalization transfers. In Germany, the Bundesrat and its committees, because of the unique character of this federal second legislative chamber composed of the delegates of the Land executives, has played a key role in intergovernmental deliberations relating to the adjustment of the financial arrangements. In other federations, including Switzerland and Belgium, periodic commissions have from time to time advised governments on the adjustment of intergovernmental financial arrangements.

Chapter 5

Processes for Flexibility and Adjustment in Federations

5.1 IMPORTANCE OF PROCESSES FOR INTERGOVERNMENTAL COLLABORATION

The inevitability within federations of overlaps and interdependence in the exercise by governments of their powers has generally required the different orders of government to treat each other as partners. This has required extensive consultation, cooperation and coordination between governments.

The institutions and processes for intergovernmental collaboration serve two important functions: conflict resolution and a means of adapting to changing circumstances.

Intergovernmental relations have two important dimensions. They may involve relations between the federal and unit governments and inter-unit relations. Typically in federations both have played an important role.

Within each of these dimensions relations may commonly involve all the constituent units within the federation, regional groupings of units, or be bilateral (i.e. between the federal government and one regional unit or between two regional units).

5.2 FORMS AND EXTENT OF INTERGOVERNMENTAL RELATIONS

An important element of intergovernmental relations that occurs within federations is carried out informally through various means of direct communications (e.g. by letter and telephone), between ministers, officials and representatives of different governments with each other.

In addition to these there are in most federations a range of more formal institutions to facilitate intergovernmental relations, such as those we have already noted in section 4.8 above relating to financial relations. These have usually taken the form of a variety of standing and ad hoc meetings involving ministers, legislators, officials and agencies of different governments. A noteworthy feature is the prevalence of "executive federalism," i.e. the predominant role of governmental executives (ministers and their officials), in intergovernmental relations in parliamentary federations where responsible first ministers and cabinet ministers tend to predominate within both levels of government.[15] The institutions and processes of executive federalism have usually developed pragmatically rather than by constitutional requirement, but in such federations as Canada, Australia, Germany, India and Malaysia they range extensively from meetings of officials to councils of ministers and to first ministers' meetings. Within some federations there have been over five hundred such committee, council and conference meetings a year. These meetings have provided institutional processes for consultation, negotiation, cooperation and, on occasion, joint projects. Not uncommonly, where executive federalism has been the characteristic mode of intergovernmental relations, governments have each established their own internal specialized intragovernmental organizations to coordinate their relations with other governments within the federation. A recent development in Australia has been the establishment in 1992 of the Council of Australian Governments to oversee the collaborative process and particularly to make the operation of the Australian economic union more effective. Among contemporary federations executive federalism in intergovernmental relations is probably the most extensively developed in Australia and Germany, with the Bundesrat serving as the centrepiece in the latter.

Where there has been a separation of legislative and executive powers within each government of a federation, as in the United States and Switzerland, channels for intergovernmental relations have been more dispersed. These have involved a variety of channels between executives, administrators and legislators in different governments often in crisscrossing patterns. A notable feature has been the extensive lobbying of federal legislators by various state and cantonal representatives.

The need for extensive intergovernmental relations has been further increased in those federations where there is a constitutional requirement that a considerable portion of federal legislation must be administered by the governments of the regional units. This has been a major factor contributing for example to the "interlocked federalism" for which Germany is especially noted.

As already noted in section 4.8, in most federations intergovernmental institutions and processes have been particularly important for the regular adjustment of financial arrangements and transfers.

In virtually every federation intergovernmental relations have had both vertical and horizontal dimensions. In addition to relations between the federal and constituent unit governments there have been inter-unit relations. These have often dealt with cross-boundary issues affecting neighbouring states or provinces, for example jointly shared rivers, transportation routes or environmental issues. In addition there are often efforts by regional groupings of states or provinces to cooperate. Sometimes inter-unit efforts at cooperation have been extended even more broadly to encompass all the states or provinces within a federation to deal cooperatively with issues of wider scope without resort to the centralizing impact of relying on federal government action. Such efforts in Switzerland have been referred to as "federalism without Bern" and in the United States as "federalism without Washington." These efforts have generally had limited success because of the confederal character of decision making involved. The successes and difficulties of these examples elsewhere are worth more extensive analysis given the recent advocacy by a number of Canadian provincial leaders that federation-wide standards in areas of exclusive provincial jurisdiction, such as health, education and social programs, be established by inter-provincial agreement rather than by federal imposition through conditions attached to federal grants.[16]

5.3 OTHER DEVICES FOR FLEXIBILITY AND ADJUSTMENT IN THE DISTRIBUTION OF POWERS

In most federations, the distribution of powers between the federal and regional unit governments is embodied in a relatively rigid constitution which is difficult to amend (see section 10.4). This has required the resort to a variety of devices for flexibility and adjustment.

In those federations such as the United States, Australia, India and Malaysia where the constitution sets out extensive areas of concurrent jurisdiction this has provided a degree of flexibility and cooperation in areas of shared jurisdiction. It should be noted, however, that concurrency can also contribute to intergovernmental competition and conflict when processes for partnership in these areas are not developed.

Another device is that of intergovernmental delegation of powers. The earlier federations did not expressly provide for this and as a result courts have sometimes limited the scope for delegation of legislative powers. Australia and most of the federations created in the twentieth century have enhanced their flexibility by including express constitutional provisions enabling delegation of legislative as well as administrative authority in either direction.

Yet another device for flexibility is the concept of "opting out" or "opting in" to the exercise of certain legislative powers. In the Canadian *Constitution Act, 1867*, sections 94A relating to pensions and survivors benefits and 94 relating to uniform property and civil rights provide examples of these. Another Canadian example of the latter is section 23(1)(a) of the *Charter of Rights and Freedoms* relating to certain minority educational rights in Quebec. Elsewhere similar provisions available to all constituent units but enabling *de facto* asymmetry have existed in Spain and Belgium.

In a number of federations, the practice of formal intergovernmental (federal-state or inter-state) agreements and accords has been developed. This has been a subject much discussed in recent decades in Canada where the Macdonald Commission advocated the inclusion of a provision allowing for the constitutional entrenchment of federal-provincial agreements. The notion of inter-state agreements finds its origin in the United States constitution. The arrangement there permits two or more states to enter into an agreement for joint action, becoming effective upon receiving Congressional consent. Inter-state agreements have been used in a number of federations by the regional units as a way of taking joint action where there is a consensus without calling upon direct intervention by the federal government. As already noted in the preceding subsection this approach has been advocated recently in Canada as a way of preserving federation-wide standards in areas of exclusive provincial jurisdiction, such as health, education and social programs, through inter-provincial agreement rather than by federal-provincial agreement.

5.4 COOPERATIVE VERSUS COMPETITIVE FEDERALISM

The prevalence of interdependence and the need for intergovernmental institutions and processes to deal with this has led to an emphasis on "cooperative federalism" within most federations. But equally significant is the concept of "competitive federalism." Analysis indicates that there are benefits and costs associated with each approach.

"Cooperative federalism" contributes to the reduction of conflict and enables coordination, but when it becomes "interlocking federalism," to the extent experienced for example in Germany, it may lead to what Scharph has called the "joint decision trap" which reduces the autonomy and freedom of action of governments at both levels.[17] Furthermore, where "executive federalism" predominates, it may limit the role of legislatures.

Advocates of "competitive federalism," for example Albert Breton in his supplementary note to the Macdonald Commission Report in Canada, argue that just as economic competition produces superior benefits compared to monopolies or oligopolies, so competition between governments serving the same citizens is likely to provide citizens with better service.[18] He equates "cooperative federalism" with collusion directed at serving the interests of governments rather than of citizens. But "competitive federalism" to excess can lead to intergovernmental conflict and acrimony and have a divisive impact within a federation.

As with all partnerships, it would appear that a blend of cooperation and competition may in the long run be the most desirable.

5.5 IMPLICATIONS FOR THE DEMOCRATIC CHARACTER OF FEDERATIONS

Excessive "cooperative federalism" may undermine the democratic accountability of each government to its own electorate, a criticism frequently voiced about executive federalism in Germany, Australia and Canada. But while, as noted above, there is some democratic value in competition among governments to serve their citizens better, competition to excess can be harmfully divisive. As is usually the case in federations, the need for balance seems to be the keynote. It has usually been found that there needs to be a combination of cooperation to avoid the harmful effect of conflict in areas of interdependence, and of competitive bargaining among governments each aiming through autonomous action to serve better the interests of their citizens.

In these circumstances, most federations have attempted to reinforce the direct accountability of their representatives in intergovernmental negotiations through the development of procedures, processes and legislative committees within each level of government rather than by restricting intergovernmental collaboration.

Chapter 6

Symmetry and Asymmetry in Federations

6.1 POLITICAL AND CONSTITUTIONAL ASYMMETRY DISTINGUISHED

Two kinds of asymmetry among regional units may affect the operation of federations. One, which is characteristic of all federations and might be described as *political* asymmetry, arises from the impact of cultural, economic, social and political conditions affecting the relative power, influence and relations of different regional units with each other and with the federal government. The other, which exists in some but not all federations and which might be labelled *constitutional* asymmetry, relates specifically to the degree to which powers assigned to regional units by the constitution of the federation are not uniform.

6.2 EXAMPLES OF POLITICAL ASYMMETRY

Political asymmetry among full-fledged constituent units exists in every federation. Among the major factors are variations in population, territorial size, economic character, and resources and wealth among the regional units. Table 12 gives an indication of the variation in population between the largest and smallest units within the federations considered in this study in descending order of the ratio between the largest and smallest regional units. The impact of this factor lies in the relative power and influence within these federations of the larger regional units, especially where one or two dominate, and in the relative powerlessness of the smallest member units. Both can be a source of internal resentment and tension in the political dynamics within federations. A particularly serious source of tension has existed in those federations where a single unit has contained over half the federation's population, almost invariably a source of instability. Notable

TABLE 12: Asymmetry of Population of Full-Fledged Constituent Units in Federal Systems

Federal System	No. of Units	Total Population	Largest Unit	Population of Largest Unit	Population % of Federation	Smallest Unit	Population of Smallest Unit	Population % of Federation	Population of Largest to Smallest
India	25	846.303 m	Uttar Pradesh	139.112 m	16.4%	Sikkim	.406 m	.05%	342.6
European Union	15	368.067 m	Germany	81.338 m	22.1%	Luxembourg	.378 m	.10%	215.2
Switzerland	26	6.873 m	Zurich	1.179 m	17.2%	Appenzell-Inner Rhodes	.014 m	.20%	84.2
Canada	10	29.108 m	Ontario	11.004 m	37.8%	Prince Edward Island	.135 m	.46%	81.5
United States	50	265.172 m	California	31.589 m	11.9%	Wyoming	.480 m	.18%	65.8
Spain	17	38.872 m	Andalucia	6.941 m	17.9%	La Rioja	.263 m	.68%	26.4
Germany	16	81.338 m	N. Rhine-Westphalia	17.759 m	21.8%	Bremen	.683 m	.84%	26.0
Australia	6	17.657 m	New South Wales	5.959 m	33.7%	Tasmania	.472 m	2.67%	12.6
Malaysia	13	16.527 m	Perak	2.108 m	12.8%	Perlis	.176 m	1.06%	12.0
Belgium	3	10.022 m	Flemish Region	5.769 m	57.6%	Brussels	.954 m	9.52%	6.0
Austria	9	7.812 m	Vienna	1.533 m	19.6%	Burgenland	.274 m	3.51%	5.6
Czechoslovakia	2	15.6 m	Czech Republic	10.360 m	66.4%	Slovak Republic	5.264 m	33.74%	2.0
Pakistan (1957-58)	2	95.6 m	East Pakistan	51.597 m	54.0%	West Pakistan	42.215 m	44.16%	1.2

Source: Annuaire statistique de la Suisse 1996; Statistics Canada; Population Distribution and Population Estimates Branches, US Bureau of Statistics;; Australia Bureau of Statistics; Bayerisches Landesamt für Statistik und Datenverarbeitung; Statistics Finland; Statistics Sweden and D.J. Elazar, ed., *Federal Systems of the World*, 2nd ed. (London: Longman, 1994).

Note: Figures for Czechoslovakia and Pakistan are those at time of dissolution of these federations; figures for other federations are latest available from sources (1994-96).

Note: For Belgium only the three Regions are compared. If the population of the three communities is used for comparison, the ratio would be much larger since the German Community represents less than one percent of the Belgian population.

examples have been Prussia within the German confederation and subsequent federation up to the 1930s, Jamaica (with 52 percent of the population) within the abortive West Indies Federation 1958-62, East Pakistan within Pakistan prior to its secession (and Punjab Province with 56 percent of the population within Pakistan after that), Russia within the former USSR, the Czech Republic within Czechoslovakia prior to the separation of 1992, and the Flemish region within the current Belgian federation. Examples where two member provinces or states have had a preponderant influence within a federation include Ontario and Quebec in Canada (combined population 62 percent), and New South Wales and Victoria in Australia (combined population 60 percent).

By contrast with these instances of relatively large regional units within federations, as Table 12 indicates, most federations also contain among their full-fledged regional units some very small ones. Most notable in terms of the population ratio between largest and smallest units are India, the European Union, Switzerland and Canada. In some federations, the desirability of reducing asymmetry in the size of constituent regions has led to pressures for the redrawing of unit boundaries as in Nigeria (where the number of units has been progressively increased from 3 regions to 30 states and 1 territory) or in Pakistan in 1956 (where the number of provinces was reduced from four provinces to two). Among other federations where the constituent units have been reshaped are Germany during the early years of the West German Republic and in East Germany at the time of reunification. In Belgium, the federalization process of the past three decades has included the delineation of the Flemish, Walloon and Brussels Regions and of the Dutch, French and German speaking Communities. Most recently, South Africa has reconstituted its regional structure into nine provinces. In all these cases the degree of political asymmetries among the constituent units that remains (and in most cases asymmetry continues to be significant) has been the product of constitutional revision. Asymmetry in terms of the territorial size and per capita wealth of regional units within individual federations are other factors that have reinforced the picture of unit political asymmetry among the units within federations generally.

These asymmetries are politically significant for two reasons. First, they affect the relative capacity of different regional units to exercise their constitutionally assigned powers. Second, they affect the degree of a regional unit's influence within those institutions of the federal government in which representation is based on population (such as the first chambers of the legislature, to which in parliamentary federations the federal executive is responsible).

Generally speaking, some political asymmetry has existed in every federation but where it has been extreme it has been a source of tension and instability. Furthermore, political asymmetry has often induced efforts at corrective measures. These have included moderating the political influence of larger regional units at the federal level by establishing a federal second legislative chamber with representation weighted to favour smaller regional units, and assisting less wealthy regional units by redistributive equalization transfers designed to assist those units (see section 4.7 and Table 10).

6.3 EXAMPLES OF CONSTITUTIONAL ASYMMETRY

Constitutional asymmetry refers specifically to differences in the status or legislative and executive powers assigned by the constitution to the different regional units. As indicated in the introduction and in Table 2 many federations have a variety of units with relationships to the federation substantially different from that of the full-fledged units of regional governments. These have taken the form of federal capital districts, federally administered territories, or peripheral federacies and associated states.

In most federations the formal constitutional distribution of legislative and executive jurisdiction and of financial resources applies symmetrically, however, to all the full-fledged member states (i.e. to increase regional autonomy). Nevertheless, there are some instances where the constitution explicitly provides for constitutional asymmetry in the jurisdiction assigned to full-fledged member states. Where this has occurred the reason has been to recognize significant variations among the full-fledged constituent units relating to geographic size and population or to their particular social and cultural composition and economic situation.

There have been basically three approaches establishing constitutional asymmetry in the distribution of powers within federal systems. One has been to increase from the norm the federal authority (i.e. to reduce regional autonomy) in particular member states for certain specified functions within the federal system. Such arrangements have existed in India and in the short-lived Federation of Rhodesia and Nyasaland (1953-63).

The second approach has been to increase from the norm the jurisdiction of particular member states (i.e. to increase regional autonomy). The most sustained example of this approach has been the concessions made to the Borneo states when they joined the Malaysian federation in 1963. Certain matters which come under federal government jurisdiction elsewhere in the Malaysian federation, such as native laws, communications, shipping and fisheries, were made matters of exclusive state or concurrent jurisdiction in Sabah and Sarawak. Other matters, such as immigration, remained under federal authority, but in these Borneo states require state approval when they are applied to those states. In India there have been similar adjustments in constitutional jurisdiction applied to the state of Jammu and Kashmir and to some of the newer small states that contain distinct ethnic groups. Canada from the beginning has had a measure of constitutional asymmetry principally related to denominational and linguistic guarantees in education, the use of French in the legislature and the courts, and the civil law.

There is a third constitutional approach for permitting asymmetry in the jurisdiction and powers exercised by certain member states. That is one in which the constitution is formally symmetrical in giving all the member states the same jurisdiction, but includes provisions that permit member states in certain cases to "opt in" or "opt out" of these assignments. These provisions enable governments to delegate their powers to another government, or allow member governments to take up the full exercise of their autonomy at different speeds. Such arrangements retain the formal symmetrical application of the constitutional distribution of powers to all member states, but provide specific means for accommodating within that framework a *de facto* asymmetry among member states in the exercise of these powers. In Canada sections 94 and 94A of the *Constitution Act, 1867* and section 23(1)(a) of the *Charter of Rights and Freedoms* in the *Constitution Act, 1982* have been such constitutional provisions. Thus, at a practical level Quebec has enjoyed a degree of legislature asymmetry (as exemplified by the Quebec Pension Plan) and administrative asymmetry (it collects its own income tax for example). The Meech Lake Accord 1987 and the Charlottetown Agreement 1992 contained proposals for more such provisions, although these were not enacted. The Spanish approach has been to recognize variations in the pressures for autonomy in different regions by granting to each Autonomous Community its own statute of autonomy tailored to its particular set of compromises negotiated between Madrid and the regional leadership. These agreements are nonetheless set within a framework in which it is anticipated that eventually there will be less asymmetry among them.

Among the examples of federal systems not yet mentioned which have exhibited some degree of constitutional asymmetry in the application of jurisdiction are the European Union, Russia and Belgium. The European Union, in negotiating the accession of each new member, has often had to make particular concessions. Furthermore, in order to get agreement upon the adoption of the Maastricht Treaty, the European Union found it necessary to accept a measure of asymmetry in the full application of that treaty, most notably in the cases of Britain and Denmark. Perhaps the most complex current example of constitutional asymmetry within a federal political system occurs in the variety of powers the 89 component units, such as republics, oblasts, okrugs, etc., that currently constitute the Russian Federation have been able to negotiate. Within a formally symmetrical constitutional framework many of the constituent units within Russia have concluded bilateral treaties providing for asymmetrical treatment. In the Belgian Federation constitutional asymmetry exists not only in the differences in jurisdiction of the three territorial constituent Regions and the three non-territorial constituent Communities, but also in the interrelation of between Regional Councils and Community Councils.

An important factor influencing the powers and autonomy that member states in a federation are able to exercise is the constitutional allocation of financial resources. As the extensive literature on fiscal federalism has invariably emphasized, where there has been initial symmetry in the constitutional allocation of financial resources in federations it has often produced sharp variations in the wealth and fiscal capacities of their member states. Consequently, in many federations there have been efforts to reduce the corrosive effect on unity of such disparities and to enhance federal cohesion by formal schemes for the redistribution and equalization of resources among the member states (See section 4.7). Thus, redistributive asymmetrical transfers have been employed to make the fiscal capacities of the member states more symmetrical.

Proposals for constitutional asymmetry have sometimes, most notably in Canada, raised the question whether greater autonomy of jurisdiction for some member states should affect the representation of those states in the federal institutions. For example, should representatives from the more autonomous member states be restricted from voting within the federal institutions on those matters over which the federal government does not have jurisdiction in their particular member state. A rational argument can be made for such a *quid pro quo*, and the issue has recently been intensely debated in Canada as a consideration if Quebec were to be given significant asymmetric legislative authority. There would, however, be serious complexities in trying to operate a system of responsible cabinet government if cabinets had to rely on different majorities according to the subject matter under deliberation. In any case, in no federation to date have adjustments actually been made in federal representation or voting by state or provincial representatives within the federal institutions on such grounds.

Clearly constitutional asymmetry among the regional units within a federation introduces complexity. Nevertheless, some federations have found that the only way to accommodate the varying pressures for regional autonomy has been to incorporate asymmetry in the constitutional distribution of powers. The most notable such cases being Malaysia, Canada, India and Belgium. In some other cases, asymmetry has proved useful as a transitional arrangement accommodating regions at different stages of political development. Examples are the arrangements within Spain for the various Autonomous Communities and the concept of a Europe of "variable geometry" proceeding at "varying speeds." In some cases pressures for asymmetry have induced counter-pressures for symmetry, for example in Canada and Spain, and there these suggest that there may be limits to asymmetry beyond which extreme asymmetry may become dysfunctional. Nevertheless, in a number of federations it appears that the recognition of constitutional asymmetry has provided an effective way of accommodating major differences between constituent units.

Chapter 7

Multilevel Federal Systems

7.1 THE IMPACT OF MEMBERSHIP IN SUPRA-FEDERATION FEDERAL ORGANIZATIONS

A notable feature in the contemporary world is the membership of a number of federations within wider federal organizations. One particular example is the membership of Germany, Belgium, Austria and Spain in the European Union. Membership in the European Union, itself a hybrid which is predominantly confederal in character but has some of the characteristics of a federation, has had implications for the internal relationships within those European Union member states which are themselves federations. Among the issues that have arisen has been the role of the regional units within each of these federations in negotiations with the institutions of the European Union. This has led to the establishment by regional units within the member federations of offices at the European Union capital in Brussels and to their direct representation in the Committee of Regions of the European Union. This has introduced a new element of complexity into intergovernmental relations in these federations. The impact upon the federal-regional balance within each federation of the transfer of certain powers to Brussels has also on occasion become a contentious issue, most notably in Germany where it led to an important case before the German Constitutional Court. It should also be noted that concern about the impact of membership in the European Union upon the character of the Swiss federation has been a factor in resistance within Switzerland to joining the European Union.

Other illustrations of federations in wider supra-federation organizations are the membership of Canada, the United States, and Mexico (all three themselves federations) within the North American Free Trade Area (NAFTA), Malaysia in the Association of South East Asian Nations (ASEAN), and of India and Pakistan (both currently federations) in the South Asian Association for Regional

Co-operation (SAARC). In each of these cases membership in the wider organization has had implications for internal organization and balance within the member federations.

Traditionally, the analysis of federations has centred upon relations between their federal and state governments. But increasingly in the contemporary world, federal arrangements have taken on a multi-tiered character. It has been the effort to maximize citizen preferences or reduce their frustrations that has led to the establishment of multiple levels of federal organization each operating at a different scale for performing most effectively their particular functions. The resulting multi-tiered federal systems have created a more complicated context for the operation of individual federations participating in these wider forms of federal organization.

7.2 THE PLACE OF LOCAL GOVERNMENTS

While considering the trend to multi-tiered federal systems, it should be noted that there has been increasing attention given also to the role of local governments within federations. Traditionally, the determination of the scope and powers of local government was left in federations to the intermediate state governments. The importance and autonomy of the tier of local government has varied enormously from federation to federation being perhaps most prominent in Switzerland and the United States and least in Australia. Furthermore, in some federations intergovernmental relations directly between federal and local governments has been considerable, whereas in others (including Canada) such relations have been funnelled through the provinces or states as intermediaries. It is worth noting that in recent years there have been efforts in some federations, notably Germany and India, to recognize formally in the constitution of the federation the position and powers of local governments. In Australia, representation for local governments was formally included in the new Council of Australian Governments established in 1992 to improve collaboration on economic development policies.

Chapter 8

Degrees of Decentralization and Non-centralization in Federations

---

8.1 CONCEPTUAL ISSUES IN MEASURING DECENTRALIZATION AND RELATIVE AUTONOMY

The concepts of decentralization and non-centralization are closely related. Some authors have preferred to use the term "non-centralization" to "decentralization" in relation to federations on the grounds that the latter implies a hierarchy with power flowing from the top or centre whereas the former infers a constitutionally structured dispersion of power and represents better the character of a federation.[19] Nevertheless, since the term decentralization is in such widespread public use, the terms will be used interchangeably here.

While in ordinary language we may loosely compare differing degrees of decentralization within federations, the comparative measurement of decentralization or non-centralization is actually a complex issue. There are at least four problems in discussing the degree of decentralization (or centralization) within a political system: first, how to define what the concept of decentralization actually refers to; second, how to measure it; third, how to relate different indices of measurement to each other; and fourth, how to compare such measurements across countries or over time.

To begin with we must distinguish between decentralization of jurisdiction, i.e. the responsibilities exercised by each level of government, and decentralization of decision making at the federal level, i.e. the degree to which the constituent units play a significant role in decision making at the federal level. The former, decentralization of jurisdiction, has itself two aspects to be distinguished: the *scope of jurisdiction* exercised by each level of government, and the *degree of autonomy* or freedom from control by other levels of government with which a particular government performs the tasks assigned to it. For example in one sense Japan (a decentralized unitary state) is highly decentralized in terms of the administrative tasks performed by the prefectures and the local authorities, but in another sense it is relatively centralized in terms of the controls the central government exercises over these subordinate levels of government. Some federations allocate fewer responsibilities to their constituent states or provinces, but leave them with greater freedom and autonomy over the exercise of those responsibilities.

A major problem in any comparative assessment is that no single quantifiable index can adequately measure the scope of effective jurisdictional decentralization and the degree of autonomy of decentralized decision making within a political system. Among the multiple indices, although not all of equal weight, that need to be considered in any such assessment are the legislative and administrative decentralization, financial decentralization, decentralization to non-governmental agencies, constitutional limitations, and the character of federal decision making. Each of these indices is discussed.

Legislative Decentralization

- The formal allocation by the constitution of legislative powers to each level of government gives an indication of the scope of decentralized jurisdiction. Appendix A provides a tabulation for various federations. In comparing such allocations in different federations, however, it should be noted that the relative lengths of the lists of heads of federal or state powers by themselves do not give a full picture because individual heads of power may vary in relative significance. Furthermore, account must be taken of the degree to which in practice constitutionally assigned powers are actually fully or only partially exercised by the governments to which they are assigned. Nevertheless, the constitutional allocation of legislative jurisdiction is one major indicator of the scope of jurisdictional decentralization.

- Account must be taken also of the degree of autonomy with which a government may exercise the legislative jurisdiction assigned to it by the constitution. In this respect the extent of exclusive jurisdiction and the extent of concurrent or shared responsibilities set out in the constitution is significant. Appendix A therefore indicates for each federation the extent to which each field of jurisdiction is exclusively assigned to one level of government, concurrent or shared.

- Another aspect of the autonomy of legislative decentralization is the extent to which constituent units are bound by international treaties negotiated by the federal government in areas that normally come under the jurisdiction of the constituent units. In some federations this is a limitation upon state autonomy (e.g. USA, Switzerland and Australia) but in others such federal treaties require implementing state or provincial legislation or the consent of provincial or state governments (e.g. Canada, Germany and Austria) or non-binding consultation of state governments (e.g. India and Malaysia). The Belgian federation goes furthest in giving constituent units specific powers to negotiate international treaties in areas of their own competence.

Administrative Decentralization

- The allocation of administrative responsibilities assigned by the constitution or developed through delegation or intergovernmental agreements is another relevant index of the scope of jurisdictional decentralization. While in many federations the constitutional allocation of administrative responsibilities broadly corresponds to the constitutional legislative jurisdiction there are many exceptions to this. Indeed, in most European federations their constitutions require a substantial portion of federal laws to be administered by the states. Thus, in these cases these federations are more decentralized administratively than legislatively. The same arrangement has also been applied to the European Union.

- The relative sizes of the public services of each level of government is another indicator of the scope of decentralization of decision making particularly in relation to administrative responsibilities, although it provides little indication of the degree of autonomy.

- In assessing the degree of autonomy in the exercise of administrative jurisdiction, one needs to take account of the extent to which one level of government may be dependent on another for implementing its policies (especially where a federal government is dependent upon constituent governments for this) and the degree to which one level of government which has legislative responsibilities may give direction to another government administering its legislation. It is significant, for example, that in Switzerland the cantons have extensive autonomy in how they implement federal laws for which the constitution has given them administrative responsibility, thus emphasizing the decentralized character of that federation. In other federations where administration of federal laws is delegated by the choice of the federal government rather than by constitutional requirement, the terms of the arrangement (including financial terms) and the directives of the federal government may limit the degree of autonomy with which the delegated administration is performed.

Financial Decentralization

- Federal government revenues before transfers as a percentage of all government expenditures (federal-provincial-local) provide one measure of the scope of financial centralization or decentralization. Since this relates to revenues directly raised by each level of government and excludes transfers it also provides a measure of the degree of their financial autonomy. Table 7 provides a comparative tabulation in descending order from the more centralized to the more decentralized.

- Federal government expenditures after transfers as a percentage of all government expenditures (federal-provincial-local) gives a measure of the scope of centralization or decentralization of expenditure and of the administration of programs and delivery of services. Since it includes expenditures funded by transfers it is not a good indicator, however, of the degree of financial autonomy. Table 8 provides a comparative tabulation of expenditures after transfers also in order of relative decentralization.

- The size and character (whether conditional or unconditional) of transfers from one level of government to another gives some indication of the degree of dependency or autonomy with which levels of government perform their responsibilities. Table 9 provides a comparative tabulation indicating intergovernmental transfers as a percentage of provincial or state revenue, and section 4.6 discusses the significance of conditional and unconditional transfers in different federations.

- The extent to which one level of government may and actually does use its spending power to act or influence activities in areas of responsibility constitutionally assigned to other levels of government must also be taken into account in assessing both the scope and degree of autonomy applying to decentralization within a particular political system.

- Access of constituent units to public borrowing is another indicator of the degree of financial autonomy. Provided their governments are not mired in debt, autonomy of constituent units is enhanced when they have direct and unhindered access to borrowed funds. Federations differ widely in terms of the formal or practical ability of constituent units to borrow. In some federations (e.g. Austria, India and Malaysia) the federal constitution limits foreign borrowing to the federal government. In the United States there are balanced budget requirements in many states. In Australia the constitutionally established intergovernmental Loans Council is a coordinating body with binding authority upon both levels of government. Such cases contrast with other federations including Canada where constituent units have substantial and unhindered access to both domestic and international borrowing.

Decentralization to Non-governmental Agencies

- The scope and extent of decentralization to non-governmental agencies as opposed to other levels of government is also relevant in judging the character and scope of non-centralization within a political system.

Constitutional Limitations

• Constitutional prohibitions (e.g. the *Charter of Rights and Freedoms*) prohibiting certain activities by any level of government must also be taken into
account in measuring the extent of non-centralization.

• In some federations the extent of the autonomy of both levels of government
(e.g. Switzerland) or of the states (e.g. some states in the U.S.A.) may be
subject to the checks and balances of citizen-initiated referendums.

The Character of Federal Decision Making

• In addition to the above indicators which provide various measures of decentralization in terms of the scope and autonomy of jurisdiction, the extent to
which federal decision making requires involvement of other levels of government in a co-decision-making process (e.g. the German Bundesrat) is
another measure of the degree to which policy making is decentralized. A
related factor here too is the political party structure and the degree to which
federal parties are distinct from or dependent upon provincial or state party
structures.

The assessment of the degree of decentralization within a political system is
further complicated by difficulties of quantification when measuring powers, degrees of dependency or autonomy, relative roles in areas of overlap and
interdependence, or influence upon other governments. In many federations where
the distribution of responsibilities among provincial or state governments is not
uniform, one needs also to take account of differences (i.e. asymmetry) in the
powers assigned or exercised by different constituent units and in the resources
and expenditures available to them.

Thus, it is clear that attempting to measure with any precision the degree of
decentralization (or centralization) within political systems is complicated and
difficult and at the very least requires reference to multiple indices with some
effort to weigh their relative importance.

8.2 A COMPARATIVE ASSESSMENT IN RELATION TO CANADA

Given the complex issues identified in the preceding section, an assessment of the
degree of decentralization within the Canadian federation compared with that of
other federations would require intensive and extensive research in terms of the
various indices noted above. Much of that research has yet to be undertaken by
comparative scholars. Nonetheless, it is possible to make two sets of broad objective generalizations.

First, in terms of a number of specific indices, it is clear that compared to other federations Canada is in some respects more decentralized and in other respects less decentralized. For example, in terms of the distribution of legislative powers and their exercise, in a wide range of specific areas there is at least one other federation where that specific responsibility is allocated or performed in a more decentralized way than in Canada (for a tabular summary see Appendix A). Among these examples where Canada is less decentralized in terms of the allocation of legislative jurisdiction are: language policy and culture (Switzerland and Belgium), foreign treaties (Belgium and Germany), citizenship (Switzerland and Germany), banking (U.S.A., Australia and Germany), broadcasting (Australia and Germany), criminal law (U.S.A. and Australia), energy and environment (Belgium), unemployment insurance (U.S.A., Switzerland, Australia and Germany) and the residual power (U.S.A., Switzerland, Germany and Austria). Other specific areas which are more decentralized in some other federations include defence, trade and commerce, bankruptcy, agriculture, organization of courts, police, prisons, social polices, scientific research.

In respect to the implementation of international treaties, Canada is, nevertheless, among the more decentralized. In the United States, Switzerland and Australia, for example, constituent units are bound by international treaties negotiated by the federal government in areas that would otherwise constitutionally fall under the jurisdiction of the constituent units. In Canada the autonomy of the provinces has been protected, as a result of judicial review, from such encroachment by the requirement of implementation by provincial legislation in such cases. There are other federations, such as Germany, that require the consent of state governments for treaties that affect the jurisdiction of constituent units, or that require, as in India and Malaysia, non-binding consultation of state governments before such treaties are entered into. Two federations, Germany in relation to cultural matters and Belgium more extensively, actually give to their constituent units international treaty-making powers.

One feature that particularly marks off the distribution of legislative jurisdiction in Canada and to a large extent Switzerland is that responsibilities assigned to the provincial and cantonal governments are generally in terms of exclusive jurisdiction, emphasizing their autonomy. In many other federations both the federal and constituent units have fewer exclusive powers and there is a larger area of concurrent or shared jurisdiction where ultimately federal legislation may prevail if that government so chooses.

In terms of allocation of administrative responsibilities, in Canada these generally coincide with the allocation of legislative responsibilities, criminal law being the major exception. In some other federations, notably Switzerland, Germany and India, while the general balance of legislative jurisdiction is less decentralized than in Canada, the constitution mandates *autonomous* cantonal or state administration of a substantial portion of federal laws (as already noted in Germany this applies to about 60 percent of federal legislation) so that in terms of administrative responsibilities those federations are more decentralized than Canada. Not surprisingly therefore, the state and cantonal public services in those federations are larger in proportion to the federal public service than is the case in Canada.

The scope of the decentralization of legislative and administrative responsibilities in various federations is reflected in the comparison of federal-state-local expenditures set out in Table 8. In this respect, that table indicates that in 1991 federal expenditure as a portion of total public expenditure was less in Canada (40.8 percent in 1991) than in the other federations except Switzerland (27.4 percent). Incidentally a comparison of the expenditure figures after transfers for each federation (set out in Table 8) with the comparable revenue figures before transfers (set out in Table 7) indicates a considerably greater degree of expenditure decentralization than revenue decentralization, Australia and India providing the widest differences.

Federal revenues before transfers, set out in Table 7, also indicate that Canada (48.2 percent in 1991) is, in terms of the extent of provincial autonomous revenue raising, more decentralized than most other federations except Switzerland. Furthermore, Table 9, which indicates the portion of provincial or state revenues represented by intergovernmental transfers, shows for 1990-91 Switzerland (21.7 percent), the United States (21.4 percent) Canada (18.3 percent) and Germany (16.7 percent) closely grouped at the lower end in terms of dependency on such transfers. Furthermore, as noted in section 4.6, if the proportion of transfers that are conditional is taken as a measure of dependency, the autonomy of Canadian provinces is less undermined by such dependency than the constituent units in most other federations, although this depends on the extent to which EPF (and now CHST) transfers are considered genuinely unconditional. In terms of full access to domestic and international borrowing, the Canadian provinces, like the constituent units of Switzerland, Germany, Belgium, Spain and those states in the United States which do not have self-imposed balanced budget requirements, have full autonomy. Countering these indicators of relative financial decentralization within the Canadian federation has been the use by the federal government of its spending power to act in or influence activity in areas of responsibility constitutionally assigned to the provinces, for example health and social services, in the interests of establishing "national standards." Such use of the federal spending power is not unique. Indeed, it is common in other federations. Nevertheless, in the Canadian case it has represented a serious centralizing counterweight to the otherwise relative autonomy of the provinces.

As to constitutional limits on the autonomy of both levels of government, section 10.5 of this study considers the role of constitutional bills of rights. The inclusion of such constitutional limitations as a brake on both federal and constituent unit governments, as in the U.S.A., Germany, India, Malaysia, Spain, Belgium and, since 1982, Canada does impose an element of non-centralization while at the same time limiting the autonomy of the governments of the constituent units. But there are variations among federations in the scope of such constitutionally defined fundamental rights and the Canadian *Charter of Rights and Freedoms* is among the most extensive, although the inclusion of the "notwithstanding clause" (section 33) provides governments at both levels with some leeway provided they are willing to face the resulting political controversy. In some federations, but not in Canada, the extent of autonomy exercised by both levels of government (e.g. Switzerland) or by the states (e.g. some states in the U.S.A.) may be tempered by being subject to the checks and balances of citizen-initiated referendums.

In terms of the degree to which federal decision making requires a significant involvement of the constituent units of government, Canada because of the parliamentary form of its federal institutions and the peculiar character of its Senate, is actually amongst the least decentralized federations in the world (see Chapter 9, The Representative Institutions of Federal Governments).

While in Canada there has been much comment about the character of "executive federalism" and the involvement of provincial leaders in major decision making, it is worth noting that some other federations carry provincial involvement in federal decision making much further. In the German Bundersrat (federal second chamber) delegates of the states instructed by their state governments hold an absolute veto on all federal legislation in areas of concurrent jurisdiction (which represents about 60 percent of total federal legislation) and a suspensive veto on the rest which are in areas of exclusive federal jurisdiction. In Switzerland over one-fifth of the members of the two houses of the federal parliament concurrently hold seats in cantonal legislatures, thus being in an especially strong position to advance cantonal viewpoints in the process of federal policy making. Furthermore, there is a strong tradition in Switzerland of consulting the cantons before any major action is undertaken by the federal government. It should also be noted that in some other federations (particularly in Switzerland, but also to a considerable degree in the U.S.A.) federal political parties are more directly dependent upon cantonal and state party organizations. These formal and party relationships mean that in such federations as Germany, Switzerland and even the United States there is a greater sense of "ownership" of the federal government by the regions than is generally felt in Canada.

The *second* broad generalization is that, difficult as it is to arrive at an overall ranking because of the different indices that have to be taken into account, Canada in terms of the scope of responsibilities and autonomy exercised by the provinces would appear on balance to be one of the more decentralized federations, although not indisputably the most decentralized. While, as identified above, there are some specific respects in which the constituent units in various other federations have had more extensive responsibilities or more autonomy or have exercised greater influence on federal policy making than the Canadian provinces, overall the Canadian provinces in terms of jurisdiction and fiscal autonomy across a wide range of policy areas of major importance to their residents have been more powerful than the constituent units in most other federations. Canada is, on balance, generally more decentralized than Australia, Austria and most of the newer Asian, African and Latin American federations and quasi-federations including India, Malaysia, South Africa and Brazil. Furthermore, one area in which Canada is clearly the most decentralized federation is in the operation of its economic union in relation to mobility of people, goods, services and capital. Indeed, it could be argued that in this respect Canada is in fact also more decentralized than the basically confederal European Union. But Canada is in at least some significant respects less decentralized than Switzerland, Belgium, Germany and the United States. Switzerland would appear to be on balance overall more decentralized than Canada, and Belgium appears to be continuing to move rapidly towards greater decentralization. On the other hand, while Germany and the United States are more decentralized than Canada in some significant major respects they are in others less so and on balance are probably best described as less decentralized than Canada. Canada certainly is nowhere near as decentralized, however, as the West Indies Federation (1958-62), the most decentralized federation of modern times in which federal revenues in 1960-61 represented only 3.5 percent of combined federal and territorial revenues.[20] Since the lack of sufficient effective federal powers contributed to the early disintegration of the West Indies Federation, that example serves, however, more as a caution about the limits to radical decentralization than as a guide to be followed.

To summarize, in comparative terms Canada is one of the more decentralized federations, but cannot be described conclusively as clearly the most decentralized federation. Furthermore, in terms of specific indices there are a considerable number of respects in which some other federations exhibit elements of greater decentralization in terms of scope and autonomy of jurisdiction or participation and influence of the constituent units in federal decision making than Canada.

This suggests that in any effort to rebalance the Canadian federation there does exist room for adjustment which could include some increased decentralization and devolution. This should be based, however, on an intelligent consideration of specific areas where adjustments in jurisdiction and in processes of federal policy making might contribute to accommodating the concerns of Quebec and of other provinces and to increased efficiency while avoiding undermining the long-term effectiveness of the federal government.

Furthermore, experience in other federations and confederations, particularly multilingual and multinational ones, suggests that some degree of "variable geometry" in the powers and responsibilities of different provinces (i.e. asymmetry) may be desirable to take account of the unique linguistic and cultural circumstances of Quebec, and the different capacities of the larger provinces like Ontario, Quebec, British Columbia and Alberta by comparison with the smallest provinces such as Prince Edward Island. But this would require Canadian political leaders to focus upon the "effectiveness" of such arrangements as the primary criterion and not merely upon "status."

8.3 MINIMUM FEDERAL POWERS

The preceding analysis in this study indicates that there is an enormous variation among federations both in terms of the degree of centralization or decentralization regarding particular functions and in general. This raises the question whether experience elsewhere suggests that there is a minimum list of federal powers required if a federation is to be effective over the long term.

In addressing this question it should be noted that the essence of federal political systems is to reconcile diversity and unity within a single political system by assigning sovereignty over certain matters to the constituent provinces and sovereignty over other matters to the federal government with each level of government responsible directly to its electorate. Any consideration of devolving additional powers to the provinces must, therefore, involve taking account of what powers may be required for the federal government to fulfil its role for the federation as a whole. Decentralization and devolution of powers that may be desirable to accommodate linguistic, cultural, historical and economic diversity or to enhance administrative efficiency will not by themselves hold a federation together. All federations need a central focus of loyalty able to deal effectively with matters of common interest if the federation is to hold the loyalty of its citizens over the long term.

Experience in other federations suggests that although there have been many variations in terms of the precise formulation, federal governments have generally been assigned the major responsibility for defence, international relations, currency and debt, and equalization, and the primary (although not exclusive) responsibility for management of the economy and the economic union.

Provinces or states have usually been given exclusive or primary responsibility for education, health, natural resources, municipal affairs and social policy. Areas such as agriculture, environment, immigration, language and culture have often been shared through some form of concurrency, legislative delegation or intergovernmental agreements. However, in some multicultural or multinational federations (e.g. Switzerland and Belgium) constituent governments have been given a primary responsibility for their own language policy and culture. It is also worth noting that in a number of federations provisions for *de facto* and even *de jure* asymmetry in the powers of particular constituent units has been provided for (e.g. Belgium, Malaysia, India, Spain, and Russia, and also the European Union).

Chapter 9

The Representative Institutions of Federal Governments

9.1 THE IMPORTANCE OF SHARED FEDERAL INSTITUTIONS AS A FOCUS FOR UNITY

There are two essential aspects in the design and operation of any federation: the recognition of diversity through a constitutional distribution of powers which enables the self-rule of the constituent units in specified areas of jurisdiction (considered in section 8.3) and the shared institutions of federal government which enable common action and provide the glue to hold the federation together (considered in this section). With respect to the shared institutions of federal government, experience in federations generally suggests that to obtain the confidence of the citizens in the different units, two criteria must be met: (1) representativeness within the institutions of the federal government of the internal diversity within the federation, and (2) effectiveness in federal government decision making.

The shared institutions of a federation are different in character from those in a confederation. In a confederation the common institutions are composed of the delegates appointed by and accountable to the *constituent governments*. In a federation the common institutions are composed mainly of representatives directly elected by and accountable to the *citizens* and in exercising its legislative and taxing powers the federal government normally acts directly on the citizens. One advantage that federations have over confederations is that by the direct relationship of their federal governments to the citizens, paralleling the direct relationship of the regional governments to their electorates, they minimize the "democratic deficits" and technocracy that have characterized contemporary confederal political systems, in which the central institutions are not directly elected but are composed of officials and ministers who serve as delegates of the constituent governments. This "indirect" relationship with the electorate of the central confederal institutions has tended in practice to create difficulties for generating public support and loyalty for those institutions, a difficulty apparent for instance in the European Union.

9.2 INSTITUTIONS BASED ON THE SEPARATION OF POWERS OR PARLIAMENTARY PRINCIPLES

Generally the federal government institutions within federations fall into one of two basic categories: those embodying the separation of executive and legislative powers and those involving the fusion of executive and legislative powers in a parliamentary executive responsible to the popularly elected house of the federal legislature. The distinction between these alternatives is significant because the form of these institutions has a major impact on the political dynamics within a federation.

Each of these forms of executive-legislature relationship has a differing democratic premise. The separation of executive and legislative powers with fixed terms for each is directed at limiting the possible abuse of power. It is a further extension of the principle of dispersing powers among multiple decision-making centres which is implicit in the concept of federation itself. In federations incorporating the separation of the executive and the legislature, power is not only divided *between* federal and regional governments but also divided *within* each level of government. By contrast, the fusion of executive and legislative power in parliamentary systems is based instead on the democratic notion that by placing the executive in the legislature and making it continuously responsible to the legislature which is itself democratically controlled in elections, coherent but controlled and accountable federal policies will be possible. In federations incorporating this latter arrangement authority is *divided* between the federal and regional governments, but within each level power is *concentrated* in a parliamentary fusion of executive and legislature.

One form of executive-legislature relationship embodying the principle of the separation of powers is the presidential-congressional form exemplified by the United States in which the president and the two houses of Congress are each elected directly for a fixed term. Another is the collegial executive in Switzerland where the executive is a Federal Council elected by the federal legislature but for a fixed term, and constitutes a collegial group, rather than a single person. In this form the presidency rotates annually among its members.

There are two types of parliamentary executives: those modelled closely on the pattern of the majoritarian British institutions at Westminster as found, for example, in Canada, Australia, India and Malaysia, and those following European traditions of responsible cabinet government based on coalitions as found in

Austria, Germany, Belgium and Spain. Some federations in each of these two variants of parliamentary government are constitutional monarchies, e.g. Canada, Australia, Malaysia, Belgium and Spain, while some are republics with presidents elected either directly or by an electoral college, as in Austria, Germany and India. Despite these variations, basically common to all these parliamentary federations is a fusion of powers in which the federal cabinet is chosen from the members of the federal legislature and is accountable to it for its continued existence in office.

The examples of the basic forms of executive-legislature relationship are set out in Table 13, which refers not only to the institutions of the federal governments but also those of the regional governments in each federation.

There is a third category which might be called the hybrid presidential parliamentary form of executive. Russia is an example of a federation incorporating this form in which a directly elected president with some significant executive powers is combined with a parliamentary cabinet responsible to the federal legislature. France provides an earlier non-federal example of this form of executive-legislature relationship.

9.3 THE SIGNIFICANCE OF THESE FORMS FOR THE REPRESENTATIVENESS AND EFFECTIVENESS OF FEDERAL GOVERNMENTS

These various forms of federal government institutions have had a differing impact upon the dynamics of federal politics in these federations affecting particularly the representativeness and effectiveness of their federal governments.

They have, for instance, affected the relative roles and effectiveness of their federal executives and legislatures. The presidential-congressional form in the United States has given both the president and the two houses of Congress prominent roles and has limited the excessive dominance of either by the checks and balances on each other, but it has been prone to deadlocks and impasses, especially when different parties control the presidency and the houses of Congress. The Swiss collegial Federal Council has provided an opportunity for inclusive representativeness through multiparty maximum coalitions embracing in its membership all the major parties in the legislature. This has, however, resulted in prolonged and lengthy decision-making processes. Nevertheless, it has meant that when decisions are reached they have generally had wide public support. The parliamentary forms of executive found in the other federations have tended to provide more cohesive and decisive federal governments, but at the price of entailing strong party discipline, executive dominance and a more majoritarian emphasis by comparison with those embodying the separation of powers principle. The presidential-parliamentary hybrid, as exemplified by the Russian federation, aims at the best of both worlds, but in practice seems to have achieved

TABLE 13: Forms of Executives and Legislatures in Federations

Federation	Federal Executive-Legislature Relationship	Head of Federal Government	Head of Federation	Bicameral or Unicameral Federal Legislature	State/Provincial Executive-Legislature Relationship	Head of Regional Government	Head of Regional State
Canada	Fused: responsible cabinet	Prime Minister	Monarch (Governor General)	Bicameral	Fused: responsible cabinet	Premier	Lieutenant Governor[1]
United States	Separated: President-Congress	President[2]	President[2]	Bicameral	Separated: Governor-Legislative	Governor[2]	Governor[2]
Switzerland	Separated: Fixed-term collegial executive	President[3]	President[3]	Bicameral	Separated: Fixed term collegial executive	President of cantonal council[4]	President of cantonal council[4]
Australia	Fused: responsible cabinet	Prime Minister	Monarch (Governor General)	Bicameral	Fused: responsible cabinet	Premier	Governor[5]
Austria	Fused: responsible cabinet	Chancellor	President[2]	Bicameral	Fused: responsible cabinet	Governor	Governor
Germany	Fused: responsible cabinet	Chancellor	President[6]	Bicameral	Fused: responsible cabinet	Minister President (or Mayor)	Minister President (or Mayor)
India	Fused: responsible cabinet	Prime Minister	President[6]	Bicameral	Fused: responsible cabinet	Chief Minister	Governor[7]

Malaysia	Fused: responsible cabinet	Prime Minister	Yang di-Pertuan Agong[8]	Bicameral	Fused: responsible cabinet	Chief Minister	Hereditary Ruler or Governor[9]
Belgium	Fused: responsible cabinet	Prime Minister	Monarch	Bicameral	Fused: responsible collegial executive	President of Executive	President of Executive
Spain	Fused: responsible cabinet	Prime Minister[10]	Monarch	Bicameral	Fused: responsible council	President of Governing Council	President of Governing Council

Notes:

[1] Appointed by monarch on advice of federal government.
[2] Directly elected.
[3] Annual rotating chairman of Federal Council.
[4] Some directly elected, some elected by cantonal legislature, some elected by cantonal executive.
[5] Appointed by monarch on advice of state government.
[6] Elected by electoral assembly of federal and state legislators.
[7] Appointed by president on advice of Union government.
[8] Selected for five-year term from among hereditary rulers of nine Malay states.
[9] Hereditary rulers in nine states, governors in four states appointed by state legislative assemblies.
[10] Titled President of Government.

the worst of both. It has been characterized in Russia by complexity and tensions between the two aspects of the federal government executive.

The different forms have also affected the capacity for regional representativeness within the executive of the federal government. In terms of balancing regional and minority interests within the executive, the U.S. presidential form is limited basically to two individuals: the president and the vice-president. While most presidential candidates have taken regional balance into account in selecting their vice-presidential running mates, this has provided only a rudimentary opportunity for regional or other balancing. The collegial form in Switzerland, although limited to the seven members of the Federal Council, has in practice exhibited a much better opportunity to ensure representation not only of the four major political parties but also of the different language and religious groups and of major cantons. In this respect it is an important vehicle for expressing within the federal executive the Swiss proportionality syndrome (i.e. the insistence upon proportional representativeness of different groups in the composition of every federal body). The various parliamentary executives in the other federations have typically all been widely representative. The "proportionality syndrome" in federal cabinet composition has been strong not only in Canada but in virtually all the parliamentary federations, although party distribution within the federal legislature may moderate or constrain the scope of representation that is possible. The Russian presidential-parliamentary hybrid has enabled some representativeness in the parliamentary portion of the executive, but this has been hampered by the complex and not always clear party distribution in the Duma.

The form of executive has also affected the capacity of the federal executive to generate federal consensus. The U.S. presidential form provides a strong personal focus upon the president as federal leader. Furthermore, the need to capture the support of a majority of the electorate in presidential elections encourages electoral campaigns aimed at aggregating the widest range of possible support from different groups. On the other hand, the frequency of presidential-congressional impasses, particularly when the presidency and the houses of Congress are dominated by different parties, has often emphasized political divisions and had a corrosive impact on consensus within the federation. The collegial form of federal institutions in Switzerland has contributed to federal cohesion by inducing political processes that have emphasized maxi-coalitions and inclusiveness. On the other hand, the time taken to produce decisions through these processes has from time to time produced a measure of public frustration. The parliamentary federal executives, where based on single-party majorities or on stable coalitions (the latter being typical of the European federations) have generally contributed to cohesion. But, where cabinets are based upon the support of a simple majority in the federal legislature, they tend to be perceived as less inclusive of the variety of regional interests and minorities than in the Swiss case and to leave significant regions or groups feeling themselves inadequately represented. Canadian experience in this respect is but one example. Furthermore, in those federations where a multiparty system develops and stable coalitions are not developed, the resulting federal government instability may seriously undermine federal cohesion. The experience of Pakistan prior to the secession of East Bengal is an example, and the tensions within Belgium from time to time is another. The presidential-parliamentary hybrid from Russia has to date not been very effective in producing federal cohesion.

The form of executive within both federal and regional levels of government has also had a significant impact upon the character and processes of intergovernmental relations in federations. In the U.S.A. the presidential-congressional system at the federal level and the parallel separation of powers between governors and legislatures in the states has meant the dispersal of power within each tier of government. This has made necessary multiple channels of federal-state relations involving executives, officials, legislators and agencies interacting not only with their opposite numbers but in a web of criss-crossing relationships which one American scholar has characterized as "marblecake federalism."[21] Within this complex set of processes, Congress, and its various committees and sub-committees, has played a particularly significant role because of its part in approving the variety of specific grant-in-aid programs.

The collegial form of executive within governments at both levels in Switzerland has also led to the dispersed conduct of intergovernmental relations. Two other factors have added to this. One is the arrangement whereby the Swiss cantons are responsible for the administration of much federal legislation and therefore are extensively consulted by different branches of the federal government concerning proposed legislation. An additional channel of intergovernmental communication between legislators arises from the provisions enabling dual membership in cantonal and federal legislatures. Over one-fifth of the legislators in each federal house are in practice in this category.

In the other federations where parliamentary responsible cabinets have operated within governments at both levels, a common prevailing characteristic has been the executive predominance in intergovernmental relations (see also section 5.2). "Executive federalism" has been most marked in Germany, Australia and Canada, but is also a major characteristic of intergovernmental relations in India, Malaysia, Austria, Belgium and Spain. This is a natural outcome of the existence within both levels of government of a governmental form in which dominant cabinets and strong party discipline have been induced by the requirement of continuous support by their respective legislatures.

The presidential-parliamentary hybrid in Russia would appear so far to have led to executive dominance in intergovernmental relations due to the weakness of the legislators. An interesting feature affecting intergovernmental relations is the constitutional provision that each regional unit be represented in the federal second chamber, the Federation Council, by two representatives, one chosen by the legislature of the constituent unit and the other representing the executive of that unit.

9.4 THE IMPACT OF ELECTORAL SYSTEMS AND POLITICAL PARTIES

The particular electoral system employed for the institutions of federal government has also had an impact on the representativeness and effectiveness of these federal institutions. In the U.S.A., Canada, India and Malaysia, single-member constituency plurality electoral systems have been employed for the popularly elected first house of the federal legislature. In Switzerland, Australia, Austria and Belgium various forms of proportional representation have been used for elections to the lower house of the federal legislature. Germany employs a mixed system with half the members of the Bundestag elected by proportional representation from party lists and the other half by plurality votes in single-member constituencies.

These differing electoral systems have had an impact upon the processes for generating federal cohesion, the representation of regional and minority views, and the relative stability of governments. In federations with single-member plurality electoral systems, the inherent overrepresentation of swings in voting patterns has made them highly sensitive to shifts in electoral opinion. In the United States and Canada it has also for the most part provided stable single-party majorities. However, the inherent overrepresentation of pluralities has been at the expense of representativeness, with minority parties tending to be underrepresented. Furthermore, in some cases such as India, the degree of social diversity has produced a pattern requiring coalition governments. On the other hand, those federations employing proportional representation electoral systems have reflected voting distribution much more accurately, although since they do not exaggerate voting shifts, they are less sensitive to changes. Furthermore, they have tended to encourage multiparty systems. As a result, party coalitions have been the norm for federal governments in many of these countries and particularly Switzerland, Austria, Belgium and Germany.

An important factor in the dynamics of any federation is the character and role of its political parties. These tend to be influenced by both institutional characteristics, particularly the executive-legislative relationship and the electoral system, and by the nature and characteristics of the diversity in the underlying society. There are four aspects of political parties that may particularly affect the operation of a federation: (1) the organizational relationship between the party organizations at the federal level and provincial or state party organizations, (2) the degree of symmetry or asymmetry between federal and provincial or state party alignments, (3) the impact of party discipline upon the representation of interests within each level, and (4) the prevailing pattern of political careers.

In terms of party organization the federal parties in the United States and especially Switzerland have tended to be loose confederations of state or cantonal and local party organizations. This decentralized pattern of party organization has contributed to the maintenance of non-centralized government and the prominence in their federal legislatures of regional and local interests. In the parliamentary federations, the pressures for party discipline within each government have tended to separate federal and provincial or state branches of parties into more autonomous layers of party organization. This tendency appears to have been strongest in Canada. The ties between federal and regional branches of each party have remained more significant, however, in such parliamentary federations as Germany, Australia and India. In the case of Belgium, the federal parties have in fact become totally regional in character with each party based in a region or distinct linguistic group. This is a pattern that may possibly emerge in Canada with the recent rise of the Bloc Québécois and the Reform Party (although the latter is striving to be more than a regional party).

In virtually all of these federations there is a degree of asymmetry in the alignment of parties at the federal level and the alignments of parties within different regional units. Within regions the prevailing alignment of parties in regional politics has often varied significantly from region to region and from federal politics. These variations in the character of party competition and predominance in different regional units have usually been the product of different regional economic, political and cultural interests, but these regional variations in prevailing parties have contributed to the sense of regional identification and distinctiveness within these federations.

The pressure or absence of strong party discipline in different federations has also had an impact upon the visible expression of regional and minority interests within the federal legislatures. Where parliamentary institutions have operated, the pressure has been to accommodate regional and minority interests as far as possible behind closed doors within party caucuses so that the visible facade is one of cabinet and party solidarity. This contrasts with the shifting alliances and visibly varying positions much more frequently taken by legislators in federal legislatures where the principle of the separation of powers has been incorporated. Regional and minority concerns are more openly expressed and deliberated in the latter cases, although that has not necessarily meant that they are translated any more effectively into adopted policies.

An area that illustrates the contrasting representational patterns in different federations is the differences in the normal pattern of political careers. In some federations, most notably the United States and Switzerland the normal pattern of political careers is progression from local to state or cantonal and then to federal office. Presidential candidates in the U.S.A., for instance, have usually been selected from among governors or senators rooted in their state politics. By contrast, in Canada few major federal political leaders have been drawn from the ranks of provincial premiers and it is the norm for Canada's most ambitious politicians to fulfil their entire careers at one level or the other, in federal or in provincial politics. The political career patterns in most of the other parliamentary federations fall between these extremes, examples of the links between provincial experience and filling positions of federal office being more frequent in such federations as Germany, Australia and India than in Canada.

9.5 THE ROLE OF FEDERAL SECOND CHAMBERS

Bicameralism within Federations

The principle of bicameralism has been incorporated into the federal legislatures of most federations. Debate over whether representation in the federal legislature should be in terms of population or in terms of the states was intense at the time of the creation of the first modern federation, the United States. The issue was resolved at the Philadelphia Convention in 1787 by the Connecticut Compromise whereby a bicameral federal legislature was established with representation in one house, the House of Representatives, based on population, and representation in another house, the Senate, based on equal representation of the states with senators originally elected by the state legislatures. This ensured that differing state viewpoints would not be simply overridden by a majority of the population dominated by the larger states.

Since then most subsequent federations have adopted bicameral federal legislatures. Indeed, all ten federations listed in Table 13, without exception, have bicameral federal legislatures. Currently, the only federations among the 23 listed in Table 2 that do not have bicameral federal legislatures are Ethiopia and the United Arab Emirates.

But while most federations have found it necessary to establish bicameral federal legislatures there is enormous variation among them in the method of selection of members, the composition, and the powers of the second chamber, and consequently its role. Table 14 sets out the variations of these elements that have existed in federal second chambers. Table 15 summarizes the particular combination of elements incorporated in each of the federal second chambers in the federations reviewed in this study.

Selection of Members

There is considerable variety in the ways in which members of federal second chambers are elected or appointed. In three federations, Australia since its inception in 1901, the United States since 1913, and Switzerland (by cantonal choice eventually in all the cantons), members of the federal second chamber are directly elected by the citizens of the constituent units. Originally in the U.S.A. (from 1789 to 1912) most members of the federal second chamber were indirectly elected by the state legislatures. This is currently the case in Austria and India for most members of the federal second chamber. In Germany, the members

TABLE 14: Variations in Selection, Composition, Powers and Role of
Second Chambers in Federations

Selection	Composition	Powers	Role
1. Appointment by federal government (no formal consultation) (e.g. Canada 1867, Malaysia 40% of seats)	1. Equal "regional" representation (e.g. Canada for groups of provinces)	1. Absolute veto with mediation committees (e.g. USA, Switzerland)	1. Legislative chamber only (e.g. Canada, USA, Switzerland, Australia, Austria, India, Malaysia)
2. Appointment by federal government based on nominations by provincial governments (e.g. Canada, Meech Lake Accord proposal)	2. Equal state representation (e.g. USA, Australia, and 60% of Malaysian senate)	2. Absolute veto on federal use of concurrent powers and suspensive veto on exclusive federal powers (e.g. Germany)	2. Combined legislative and intergovernmental role (e.g. Germany, South Africa)
3. Appointment ex officio by state governments (e.g. Germany)	3. Two categories of cantonal representation (e.g. Switzerland)	3. Suspensive veto: time limit (e.g. Malaysia, Spain)	
4. Indirect election by state legislatures (e.g. USA 1789–1912, India, Malaysia 60% of seats, Austria)	4. Weighted state representation: three categories (e.g. Germany)	4. Suspensive veto: matching lower house vote to override (e.g. Germany for some)	
5. Direct election by simple plurality (e.g. USA since 1913)	5. Weighted state representation: multiple categories (e.g. Austria, India)	5. Deadlock resolved by joint sitting (e.g. India)	
6. Direct election by proportional representation (e.g. Switzerland de facto, Australia)	6. Additional or special representation for others including aboriginals (e.g. Malaysia, India)	6. Deadlock resolved by double dissolution then joint sitting (e.g. Australia)	
7. Choice of method left to cantons (e.g. Switzerland)		7. Money bills: brief suspensive veto (e.g. India, Malaysia, Germany)	
8. Mixed (e.g. Malaysia, Belgium, Spain)			

TABLE 15: Selection, Composition and Powers of Federal Second Chambers

Canada	Senate: appointed by federal government + equal regional representation for groups of provinces (some exceptions) + absolute veto (legally).
United States	Senate: direct election since 1913 (by simple plurality) + equal state representation + absolute veto (mediation committees).
Switzerland	Council of States: direct election (by proportional representation; chosen by cantons) + cantons with either one or two representatives + absolute veto (mediation committees).
Australia	Senate: direct election (by proportional representation: Single Transferable Vote + equal state representation + absolute veto (but followed by double dissolution and joint sitting).
Austria	Bundesrat: elected by state legislatures + weighted representation (range 12–3) + suspensive veto (may be overridden by simple majority in lower house, the Nationalrat).
Germany	Bundesrat: state government ex officio delegations + weighted representation (3–6 per state) + suspensive veto on federal exclusive powers (40% of federal legislation) overridden by corresponding lower-house majority, and absolute veto on concurrent powers (60% of legislation) with mediation committees.
India	Rajya Sabha (Council of States): elected by state legislatures (plus small number of additional representatives for special representation) + weighted representation (range 86–12) + veto resolved by joint sitting.
Malaysia	Dewan Negara (Senate): 60% elected by state legislatures (plus 40% additional appointed representatives for minorities) + equal state representation (for 6% of total seats) + suspensive veto (six months).
Belgium	Senate: combination of directly elected (40), indirectly elected (21) and coopted senators (10) + variable representation specified for each unit + equal competence with House of Representatives on some matters but on others House of Representatives has overriding power.
Spain	Senate: 208 directly elected members and 49 regional representatives + categories of 4, 3 or 1 senator each supplemented by representation related to population + suspensive veto (2 months).

of the Bundesrat are delegates of their Land cabinets, holding office in the federal second chamber ex officio as members of their Land executive and voting in the Bundesrat in a block on the instructions of their Land governments. In Canada, senators are appointed by the federal prime minister and hold office until their retirement at 75. The federal second chambers in Malaysia, Belgium and Spain have a mixed membership. In Malaysia 60 percent of the Senate seats are filled by indirect election by the state legislatures and 40 percent by central appointees. In Belgium 40 senators are directly elected, 21 indirectly elected and 10 are coopted appointees. The Spanish senate has 208 directly elected members and 49 regional representatives.

In those federations where the members of the federal second chamber are directly elected, generally they are representative of the interests of the regional electorates. Where they are indirectly elected by state legislatures they are also generally representative of regional interests although regional political party interests also play a significant role. Where, as in the German case, they are ex officio instructed delegates of the constituent governments, it is primarily the views of those governments that they represent and only indirectly those of the electorate. Where senators are appointed by the federal government, as in Canada, they have the least credibility as spokespersons for regional interests, even when they are residents of the regions they represent. Federal appointment does, however, provide a means for ensuring representation of some particular minorities and interests, and it was for that reason that the Indian constitution provided for 12 such appointed members out of a maximum total of 250 members in the Rajya Sabha and the Malaysian constitution currently provides for 42 out of 110 senators to be appointed by the federal government. The mixed basis of selection of senators in Belgium and Spain represent political compromises intended to obtain the benefits of the different forms of selection for members of the federal second chamber.

Basis of Regional Representation

In only two of the federal second chambers in the ten federations under consideration in Tables 14 and 15 are the states equally represented. These are the United States and Australian senates. In the Malaysian senate the seats filled by indirectly elected senators are equally distributed among the states, but the substantial proportion that are filled by centrally appointed senators have not followed a consistent pattern of balanced state representation, thus the net effect has been one of considerable variation in state representation. In most other federations the population of the units is a factor in their representation in the federal second chamber, although in most cases there is some weighting to favour the smaller units. There have been various degrees of weighting. In Switzerland there are two categories of representation in the Council of States: 20 cantons have 2 representatives and 6 "half-cantons" have only one each. In Germany there are three population categories of Länder having three, four or six members in the Bundesrat. In India, Austria and Spain the range of state representation is wider: for example, 86-12 in India and 12-3 in Austria. In Belgium the differential representation of each Community and Region in the senate is specified in the constitution. Canada, as is the case with so much about its Senate, is unique among federations in basing Senate representation on regional groups of provinces with the four basic regions having 24 seats each, plus an additional 6 for Newfoundland and 2 for the Territories.

Powers of Second Chambers Relative to the First Chamber

Where there is a separation of powers between the executive and the legislature, as in the U.S.A. and Switzerland, normally the two federal legislative houses have had equal powers (although in the U.S.A. the Senate has some additional powers relating to ratification of appointments and treaties). Where there are parliamentary executives, the house that controls the executive (invariably the first chamber) inevitably has more power. In these federations the powers of the second chamber in relation to money bills are usually limited. Furthermore in the case of conflicts between the two houses provisions for a suspensive veto, for joint sittings where the members of the second chamber are less numerous, or for double dissolution have usually rendered the second chamber weaker (see Table 14 column three for examples). This has sometimes raised questions within parliamentary federations about whether their second chambers provide sufficient regional influence in central decision making. This concern is reinforced by the usual strength of party discipline within parliamentary federations. Nonetheless, some of the federal second chambers in parliamentary federations, such as the Australian Senate and the German Bundesrat, have been able to exert considerable influence. The particular membership of the German Bundesrat and the fact that its absolute veto over all federal legislation in areas of concurrent jurisdiction has in practice applied to more than half of all federal legislation has been a major factor in its influence.

The primary role of most of the federal second chambers in the federations reviewed in this study has been legislative, reviewing federal legislation with a view to bringing to bear upon it regional and minority interests and concerns. By contrast with the others, the German Bundesrat performs an additional and equally important role of serving as an institution to facilitate intergovernmental cooperation and collaboration. It is able to do this because, unlike the other federal second chambers, as noted, it is composed of instructed delegates of the Land governments and because its suspensive veto power over all federal legislation and absolute veto over federal legislation affecting state legislative and administrative responsibilities give it strong political leverage. This model has heavily influenced the South Africans in the design of their national second chamber in the new constitution adopted in May 1996. From time to time during the past two decades the reform of the Canadian Senate to serve such a dual role as a House of the Provinces has been suggested. Countering this, however, has been the advocacy in the less populous provinces of a Triple-E Senate (Elected, Equal and Effective) for which the closest model in a parliamentary federation would be the Australian model. What is clear is that, of all the federal second chambers, the Canadian Senate has the least public legitimacy. But while most Canadians agree that it should be reformed, disagreement about the appropriate reform has left it unreformed.

Chapter 10

Constitutional Supremacy in Federations

10.1 THE CONSTITUTION AS SUPREME LAW

Since an essential characteristic of federations is the constitutional distribution of powers between two or more orders of government, an important feature in the design and effective operation of any federation is ensuring the supremacy of the constitution as the source of governmental authority for each order of government. A recognition of the supremacy of the constitution over all orders of government and a political culture emphasizing the fundamental importance of respect for constitutionality are therefore prerequisites for the effective operation of a federation. If these are lacking a federation is likely to deteriorate to a situation where one or other order of government subordinates the other thereby undermining the basic constitutional coordinacy which is an essential feature of federations.

The constitutions of most federations therefore explicitly or implicitly declare the supremacy of the constitution. This helps to explain why judicial review by the courts, discussed below, has been an important element in the operation of federations. Other important implications flow from the principle of constitutional supremacy in federations. These relate to the processes of constitutional amendment, the role of constitutional bills of rights, and provisions, if any, for formal secession.

10.2 PROCESSES FOR CONSTITUTIONAL ADJUDICATION AND JUDICIAL REVIEW

Given the unavoidability of overlaps and interdependence between governments within federations and the consequent likelihood of intergovernmental competition and conflict, most federations have found the need for processes to adjudicate disputes and resolve conflicts. A fundamental question that arises is whether electoral or judicial processes should be the primary means for dealing with disputes and conflicts. Most federations have in fact relied on a combination of these processes. Ultimately, through the periodic elections that occur within both levels of government in federations, electorates have had the opportunity where there is a conflict between governments to express and support their preferences by voting parties in or out of power at each level of government. In the case of Switzerland, in addition to elections at each level of government, the electorate plays a major adjudicating role through the operation of the legislative referendum. In this process any federal legislation that is challenged by 50,000 citizens or eight cantons must be submitted to a direct popular vote in a referendum. As a result this referendum process becomes the adjudicative process for ruling on the validity of federal legislation. An interesting by-product of this constitutional procedure is the inducement that it provides for interparty compromise and cohesion within the federal government and legislature in order to ensure the maximum possible breadth of support with the aim of reducing the risk of a successful challenge through the legislative referendum process.

In addition to elections within each level of government, most federations have also relied upon the courts to play a major adjudicating role. In this role courts have performed three functions: (1) impartial constitutional interpretation, (2) adaptation of the constitution to changing circumstances (especially where constitutional amendment is difficult), and (3) resolution of intergovernmental conflicts.

10.3 SUPREME COURTS AND CONSTITUTIONAL COURTS

Two types of courts for ultimate constitutional jurisdiction may be found among federations. One is a supreme court serving as the final adjudicator in relation to all laws including the constitution. Examples are the Supreme Courts of the United States, Canada, Australia, India, Malaysia and Austria. The other is a constitutional court, specializing in constitutional interpretation, which is the pattern followed in Germany, Belgium and Spain. A third approach is that found in Switzerland involving a limited tribunal. Under the unique Swiss arrangement the Federal Tribunal may rule on the validity of cantonal laws but not of federal laws. The validity of federal laws is determined instead through the instrument of the legislative referendum referred to above.

If courts are to be accepted within a federation as impartial and independent adjudicators there appear to be two requirements: (1) independence from influence on the court by any particular level of government, and (2) proportional representativeness of membership on the court. The first of these raises the issue of the method of appointment. In most federations some provision is made either by constitutional requirement or in practice for the constituent unit governments to have a role in the appointment of judges adjudicating the constitution. In the U.S.A., appointments to the Supreme Court rest solely with the president, but require ratification by the Senate where the state electorates are equally represented. In Canada and Australia constitutionally the power to appointed judges to the Supreme Court lies solely with the federal government but by convention provincial or state governments are consulted. In India and Malaysia the federal cabinet has had the last word in the appointment of Supreme Court judges but has been required by the constitution to consult certain bodies before making the appointments. In Germany the Bundesrat representing the Länder appoints half the members of the Constitutional Court and the Bundestag the other half. In Spain the Constitutional Court is composed of 12 members of whom 4 are elected by Congress, 4 by the Senate, 2 are appointed on the proposal of the Government Council, and 2 are appointed on the proposal of the General Council of Judicial Power. On the other hand, in Belgium, the members of the ultimate adjudicating Court of Arbitration are simply elected by the multi-party Federal Assembly.

The issue of proportionality in the composition of these ultimate adjudicating courts has also been an issue in most federations. This has been particularly so in Canada in relation to regional representation and especially of Quebec with its civil law tradition, in Switzerland where the three official languages are represented, and in Belgium where strict legal requirements are laid down for linguistic balance in the membership of the Court of Arbitration.

The question is sometimes raised whether federation as a form of government results ultimately in rule by judges rather than by elected representatives. There is some element of truth in this and it is reinforced where the judges also interpret a set of fundamental individual and collective rights in the constitution. This has sometimes led to the advocacy of the popular election or recall of judges, although that has not yet been applied to the most senior constitutional court in any federation. To be noted is the Swiss alternative referred to above, of the legislative referendum to determine the validity of federal laws. In this process the electorate becomes the adjudicating umpire. It should also be noted, that generally speaking, the extent to which the role of courts as adjudicators becomes prominent depends on the extent to which other methods of adjustment and conflict resolution through intergovernmental agreements, governmental changes induced by elections, and formal constitutional amendments fail to resolve problems.

10.4 CONSTITUTIONAL AMENDMENT PROCEDURES

In federations it is the constitution that defines the authority of each of the orders of government so that neither level is constitutionally subordinate to the other. It follows that the written constitution, at least in those respects defining and affecting the relative powers of the orders of government, must not be unilaterally amendable by just one order of government since that would potentially subordinate the other level of government to it. But providing for special procedures to amend the constitution raises the issue of balancing the requirements for both rigidity and flexibility in the operation of the constitution in a federation. Some element of rigidity is required to safeguard the protections built in for regional and minority interests in the constitutional structure of the federation, since a sense of regional or minority insecurity generally tends to undermine federal cohesion. At the same time it is important that as conditions change the federation is sufficiently flexible to adapt. Too rigid a constitutional structure may seriously weaken the ability of the federation to respond to and accommodate changing internal economic, social and political pressures and external international conditions. What is required then in the constitutions of federations is a balance between rigidity and flexibility.

One common means of achieving such a balance has been to provide for different amendment procedures for different parts of the constitution of a federation, with those aspects of the constitution that establish its fundamental federal character requiring the involvement of both orders of government, but the procedure for amending other portions of the constitution being more flexible. This is typical of most federations. Following this pattern, when the *Canadian Constitution Act, 1982,* (sections 38-49) added procedures for amending the Canadian constitution, five different procedures were actually set out for amending different parts of the constitution. These involve varying degrees of rigidity: (1) a "normal" procedure requiring the assent of Parliament and two-thirds of the legislatures of the provinces containing at least half the total population of all the provinces, (2) a procedure requiring the assent of Parliament and the unanimous consent of the provincial legislatures for a select number of constitutional provisions, (3) a bilateral procedure for amendment of provisions relating to some but not all provinces, (4) amendments by Parliament alone for provisions not affecting the provinces, and (5) amendments by provincial legislatures of provincial constitutions.

In most federations approval of amendments to those portions of the constitution relating to the distribution of powers and the integrity of the constituent units usually requires approval in both houses of the federal legislature (sometimes by a special majority as in the United States, India and Malaysia, otherwise by a simple majority as in Switzerland and Canada), and either approval by a special majority of the constituent unit legislatures, as in the U.S.A., Canada, India and Malaysia, or by a referendum requiring a double majority consisting of an overall majority and majorities in a majority of constituent units, as is the procedure in Switzerland and Australia.

Some special points may be noted about constitutional amendment procedures in Switzerland, Germany, Austria, Belgium and Spain. Switzerland in 1891 instituted two different procedures: one for total revision of the constitution and one for partial revision. Although attempted on a number of occasions, the former has never been successfully used, but the procedure for partial revision has been used successfully more than 110 times since 1891. There is also in Switzerland an initiative process for constitutional amendments.

Germany requires only special majorities in the two federal houses for constitutional amendments, but the Bundesrat is composed of instructed state government delegates so that endorsement by a special majority in the Bundesrat is equivalent to consent by that majority among the Land governments.

In Austria, partial constitutional amendments require passage in the lower house (Nationalrat) of the federal legislature by a two-thirds majority with at least half of the membership of the Chamber present, but one-third of the membership of either federal house may demand a total revision of the constitution requiring a referendum at which a majority of the population decides the matter.

The Belgian procedure for constitutional amendment (article 131) does not involve the Regions or Communities, but does require a complex process which involves a special election, special majorities in each federal house, and in many areas (relating to amendments to the distribution of powers or to the Court d'Arbitrage) special legislation supported by a majority of each of the two major linguistic groups in Parliament.

In Spain the initiating of constitutional amendments lies normally with the Government, Congress or Senate although there is provision for an Autonomous Community Assembly to propose constitutional amendments. Ratification is by a majority of three-fifths of the members of each federal chamber, or where the chambers disagree, by an absolute majority in the Senate and a two-thirds vote in the Congress. If one-tenth of the members of either house request it, this is followed by a referendum. A total revision of the constitution or a partial revision of certain specific portions of the constitution are more rigidly entrenched, requiring a two-thirds majority in each federal chamber and ratification by referendum.

Typically, most federations make a special attempt to protect the integrity of their constituent units by provisions in the constitution requiring the consent of a constituent unit for any modification of its boundaries.

As a result of the requirements described above, the constitutions of most federations have in practice proved relatively rigid concerning the features essential to their federal structures. Swiss and German experience points to the value of incremental partial constitutional revisions as opposed to efforts at comprehensive constitutional revision in achieving adaptation. The failure in Canada of several efforts at comprehensive constitutional revision during the past thirty years confirms this. The general rigidity of most constitutions of federations has made other forms of adjustment to achieve flexibility and adaptability all the more important. Consequently, there has been a heavy reliance in virtually all federations upon other forms of adjustment including judicial review, financial transfer arrangements, and intergovernmental collaboration and agreements.

10.5 THE ROLE OF CONSTITUTIONAL BILLS OF RIGHTS

Federations are essentially a territorial form of political organization. Thus, as a means of safeguarding distinct groups or minorities, they do this best when those groups and minorities are regionally concentrated in such a way that they may achieve self-government as a majority within a regional unit government. Examples are the many largely unilingual and uniconfessional cantons within Switzerland, the predominantly French-speaking majority in Quebec within Canada, the various linguistic majorities in the different Indian states following the reorganization of the states along linguistic lines, the distinctive populations of the Borneo states in Malaysia, the predominantly Flemish- and French-speaking regions and communities within Belgium, and the populations of the historical regions of the Basque Country, Catalonia and Galicia within Spain. In each of these cases, the primary safeguard for groups which are a minority within a federation is through their control as a majority in a self-governing regional unit having guaranteed constitutional powers within the federation.

But populations rarely in practice are distributed into neat watertight territorial regions. In virtually all federations some intra-unit minorities within the regional units of government have been unavoidable. Where significant intra-region minorities have existed three types of solutions have been attempted.

The first has been to redraw the boundaries of the constituent units to coincide better with the location of the linguistic and ethnic groups. Examples are the separation of the Jura from the canton of Bern to create a new canton, the major reorganization of state boundaries in India in 1956 and some subsequent further revisions, and Nigeria's evolution by stages from 3 regions to 30 states. While such revisions may produce more internally homogeneous and coherent regional units of government, experience makes it clear that in redrawing boundaries it is extremely difficult to avoid leaving some intra-regional minorities.

A second approach has been to assign to the federal government a special responsibility as guardian of intra-regional minorities against possible oppression by a regional majority. The Canadian *Constitution Act, 1867* included such a provision (section 93[4] relating to minority education). In India the federal government has been given a more extensive power to give direction to state governments regarding the recognition within states of minority languages, the use within states of minority languages for education, and the establishment within states of regional legislative committees and development boards. In addition provision has been made for a special officer reporting to the Union government on the operation of minority safeguards within the states. In addition the constitution gave the Union government direct responsibility to give direction to state governments regarding the scheduled areas, tribes and castes. The *Constitution of Malaya, 1957*, which preceded the later Malaysian one, gave to the federal government the power to give directions to the state governments regarding Aboriginal Peoples and also specified that changes in the reservation of land for Malays required not only a special majority in the state assembly but approval by special majorities in the federal parliament. In Pakistan prior to its separation a similar role to that in India was assigned to the federal government in relation to scheduled areas and tribes, and the authority to specify whether there would be joint or separate electorates was left under the 1956 constitution to the National Assembly to decide after consulting the provincial legislatures.

The third approach, and the most widely used one has been to protect intra-regional minorities through embodying a set of fundamental citizens' rights in the constitution. This was not the original intention of the Bill of Rights added to the U.S. constitution in the form of the first ten amendments ratified in 1791. These were intended to limit federal government action and did not initially apply to the states. Following the civil war in 1861-65 and the passage of the Fourteenth Amendment in 1868, the courts in the process of judicial review extended the protections of individual rights to apply also against state action, thus providing a protection for intra-state minorities. As set out in the constitution of the United States all such protected rights are formulated as individual rights with no provision for group rights.

A number of subsequent federations have set out in their constitutions more extensive lists of rights protected from both federal and regional government action. In some, but not all, of these cases special group rights have been included. Among the federations that have included in their constitutions a list of fundamental rights have been Germany (1949), India (1950), Malaysia (1963), Spain (1978), Canada (added in 1982) and Belgium (1993). Of these, the Basic Law of the Federal Republic of Germany lists numerous individual rights but no group rights. On the other hand, the constitutions of the multi-ethnic federations of India, Malaysia, Canada and Belgium all make provision for some group rights.

As one of the most ethnically and linguistically diverse federations, India's constitution makes provision not only for fundamental individual rights but also for the recognition and protection of linguistic minorities (including their language and education), of Anglo-Indians, and of scheduled castes and tribes. This includes provision for a "special officer for linguistic minorities" and a national commission to investigate and monitor all matters relating to the rights and safeguards of the Scheduled Castes and Scheduled Tribes.

The Malaysian constitution similarly lists individual rights and also makes special provision for certain specified groups within the states. There are explicit arrangements on behalf of the Malays for the reservation of land, for quotas for permits and for quotas for employment in the public services in the states. These guarantees have been intended to protect the Malays who, because of their relative education and economic backwardness, might otherwise suffer in competition with other racial groups, even in those states where they represent a majority. Similar provisions extend to "natives" in the Borneo states, and additional safeguards have been provided for the variety of indigenous peoples in the Borneo states centring on the continued use of native languages and the protection of the Muslim religion and education.

In Canada, the *Charter of Rights and Freedoms* added by the *Constitution Act, 1982* includes not only a wide range of individual rights but also identifies minority language rights, the rights of aboriginal peoples, and rights related to "the preservation and enhancement of the multicultural heritage."

The Belgian constitution sets out fundamental individual rights and liberties and also constitutional guarantees for linguistic minorities. As a result there are statutory guarantees concerning the use of language in administrative matters, in judicial matters, in legislation, in the armed forces, in education, in labour relations, in the bilingual capital of Brussels, and in the German-speaking region.

The Spanish constitution of 1978 sets out a long list of civil, political and socioeconomic rights, most of which are individual rights. In terms of ethnolinguistic rights the constitution specifies Castilian as the official language of Spain (article 3[1]), but also states (article 3[2]) that there may be other official languages in the respective autonomous communities, thus providing some measure of *de facto* territoriality to the language regime in Spain.

In Switzerland, Australia and Austria, however, the constitutions do not elaborate a set of fundamental rights. The Swiss constitution is mainly concerned with the organization of government structures and with the distribution of powers between the orders of government. Concerns over rights (individual or collective) receive very little treatment in the constitution. The constitution does recognize three official and four national languages and does specify that the Federal Tribunal must include representatives of all three official languages. But while the constitution contains little about rights, there have evolved a number of unwritten principles relating to linguistic rights that have come to take on considerable significance. There are three basic principles that have come to prevail considering language rights.[22] These are (1) the absolute equality of the Swiss languages, (2) cantons have general jurisdiction over language matters except where the constitution provides specific limits in favour of the federal government, and (3) the principle of "territoriality" prevails. This is interpreted to mean that "any canton or linguistic area is deemed to have the right to preserve and defend its own distinctive linguistic character against all outside forces tending to alter or endanger it."[23] This principle has been the primary guarantee for the smaller language groups and has been considered the foundation of linguistic peace in Switzerland.

Australia's constitution contains no general statement of individual or group rights although there are specific references relating to the acquisition of property on just terms, trial by jury, freedom of movement between states, freedom of religion, protection against discrimination on the basis of state residence, and voting rights. Recent jurisprudence of the High Court indicating its willingness to "imply" certain rights from the provisions of the constitution has been the subject of considerable debate.

The Austrian constitution includes no list of rights of any kind but there is a reference to minority group rights of the Croatian and Slovene minorities in article 7 of the *State Treaty of Austria, 1955* that was signed by the Allied powers and the Austrian government at the time that the occupation of Austria was ended.

10.6 PROVISIONS FOR FORMAL SECESSION

Few federations anywhere have included in their constitution the recognition of a unilateral right of secession or explicit provisions for a formal process for secession. Indeed, the constitution of the former USSR was unique in this respect being the only constitution of a federation making reference to a unilateral right of secession. Generally, three reasons have been offered for not including a unilateral right of secession in the constitutions of federations. First, it has been feared that the right to secede would weaken the whole system by placing a weapon of political coercion in the hands of the governments of the constituent units. Second, there has been anxiety that the possibility of secession would introduce an element of uncertainty and lack of confidence in the future, seriously handicapping efforts to build up federal economic development and unity. Third, theorists have argued that it would undermine the fundamental principle of coordinacy between levels of government in a federation since if a regional government acting alone had the unilateral right to leave the federation, or the federal government had the unilateral right to expel a regional unit, then the other level of government would be subordinated.

Implicitly therefore in other federations the only constitutional valid way for the secession or expulsion of a constituent unit to occur would be through the normal processes of constitutional amendment requiring endorsement by the federal legislature and the required proportion of regional units (see section 10.4). Nor has there been any inclination in federations, other than the recent discussion in Canada following the Quebec referendum in 1995, to consider publicly in advance the conditions, terms and processes under which the rest of a federation would agree to the secession of one of its constituent units. Such deliberations have been considered elsewhere as likely either to encourage or provoke sharpened sentiments for separation, and, therefore, to be avoided as likely to become self-fulfilling prophecies.

The fact that virtually all federations have made no constitutional provision for a right of unilateral secession does not mean, however, that there have not been cases of unilateral secession or expulsion. It simply means that when secession has been attempted or has occurred the process has invariably been extra-constitutional, expressing political pressures that have broken the constitutional mould. Examples will be taken up in the next section.

Chapter 11

The Pathology of Federations

11.1 SIGNIFICANCE OF THE PATHOLOGY OF FEDERATIONS

Much of the comparative literature on federal systems and federations has concentrated on their establishment and operation. Furthermore, it is true that most federations continue to be remarkably effective and that many of the longest-standing constitutional systems anywhere in the world today are federations still operating basically under their original constitutions (e.g. United States 1789, Switzerland 1848, Canada 1867 and Australia 1901). A number of authors have attributed the prosperity, stability and longevity of such federations to the effectiveness of federation as a form of political organization.[24]

But the period since 1945 has seen not only the proliferation of federal systems and particularly federations, but also the failure of some of them. Significant examples have been the disintegration of federations in the West Indies (1962), Rhodesia and Nyasaland (1963), Yugoslavia (1991), and the USSR (1991); the splitting of Pakistan (1971) and Czechoslovakia (1992); the expulsion of Singapore from Malaysia (1965); and the civil war in Nigeria (1967-70) followed by alternating civilian and military rule. In any comparative review, account must therefore be taken of these failures, of other cases of serious stress in federations that have not failed, and of the literature examining the conditions and processes leading to the breakdown of federations where this has occurred.[25] An important point to note at the outset of any consideration of the pathology of federal systems is that the problems faced by them have arisen not so much because of the adoption of federation as a form of government but from the particular variant or variation of federal arrangements that has been exclusively the source of their difficulties. In should also be noted that it is not so much because they are federations that countries have been difficult to govern but that it is because they were difficult to govern in the first place that they adopted federation as a form of government.

11.2 SOURCES OF STRESS

There are four factors that have contributed to stress within federations: (1) sharp internal social divisions, (2) particular types of institutional or structural arrange- ments, (3) the particular strategies adopted to combat disintegration, and (4) political processes that have polarized internal divisions.

The Distribution and Character of Internal Social Divisions

Regional divergences of political outlook and interests are typical of all federa- tions: that is usually why they adopted "federation" as a solution in the first place. But a number of factors may sharpen such differences. Among the sharpest divi- sive forces have been language, religion, social structure, cultural tradition and race. Where several of these have operated simultaneously to reinforce each other, as for instance in India, Malaysia, and particularly in Pakistan before its separa- tion, Nigeria, Rhodesia and Nyasaland, Yugoslavia and the USSR, the internal cleavages have been accentuated. By contrast, in Switzerland linguistic, religious and economic differences among the cantons have tended to cut across each other moderating the sharpness of internal differences. Other factors which have con- tributed to the sharpness of internal cleavages have been variations in the degree of economic development, and of regional disparities in wealth accentuating re- gional resentment, especially when these have further reinforced linguistic, cultural and social differences among regions. On the other hand, in some instances mod- erating factors which have emphasized the importance of maintaining unity have been the need for security from external threats (an important motivation in both Swiss and Canadian history but in both cases now waning in relative influence), and the significance of inter-regional trade and the need for international leverage through united action in trade and investment negotiations and relations.

The Role of the Institutions and Structures of Federations

Whether the stresses within a federation can be accommodated and resolved de- pends not only upon the strength and configuration of the internal divisions within the society in question but also upon the institutional structure of the federation. The way those institutions have channelled the activities of the electorate, politi- cal parties, organized interest groups, bureaucracies, and informal elites has contributed to the moderation or accentuation of political conflict. The function of federations is not to eliminate internal differences but rather to preserve re- gional identities within a united framework. Their function therefore is not to eliminate conflict but to manage it in such a way that regional differences are accommodated. But how well this is done has in practice depended often upon *the particular form of the institutions* adopted within the federation.

Four institutional factors have been particularly critical. First, extreme disparity in the population, size and wealth of the constituent units has invariably contributed to stress, even leading in some cases to reorganization of the boundaries of the regional units as in India and Nigeria. Almost invariably a source of instability has been the situation within a federation where one regional unit has dominated through having a majority of the population. Examples are Prussia within the German confederation and subsequent federation up to the 1930s, Jamaica within the abortive West Indies Federation 1958-62, Northern Nigeria prior to the Nigerian civil war, East Pakistan prior to its secession, Russia prior to the breakup of the USSR in 1991, and the Czech Republic within Czechoslovakia prior to its split in 1992.

Second, where the particular distribution of powers has failed to reflect accurately the aspirations for unity and regional autonomy in a given society, there have been pressures for a shift in the balance of powers or, in more extreme cases, even for abandoning the federal system, as in overcentralized Pakistan or the ineffectual West Indies Federation. It has been to avoid this extreme result that some federations such as Malaysia have instituted and maintained a constitutional asymmetry in the distribution of powers.

Third, while regional distinctiveness is a basic factor leading to the adoption of federation as a form of government, the ability of the federal institutions to generate some sense of positive consensus is vital to their continued operation. Particularly critical is how regional groups are represented in the federal legislature, executive, civil service, political parties and life of the capital city. Where particular regional groups have had inadequate representation and influence in the federal institutions, the resulting alienation has directed itself into separatist movements as in the cases of the East Pakistanis, the Singapore Chinese, the Jamaicans or the black Africans of Nyasaland and Northern Rhodesia. A particularly dangerous situation is where parties operating at the federal level have become primarily regional in their focus so that there are no federal political parties serving as effective inter-regional bridges. This was a major factor in the instability within Pakistan prior to its split in 1971, in Nigeria prior to the outbreak of civil war in 1967, in the ultimate breakdown of the Yugoslavian federation in 1991, and in Czechoslovakia in the period before it was divided in 1992. In this respect one of the most ominous signs within the current Belgian federation is the regional character of all the political parties operating at the federal level. The recent signs of a similar trend in Canada in terms of the federal opposition parties is therefore a significant danger signal.

Fourth, in most multicultural federations it has proved necessary to recognize as official the languages of major minority groups and to provide constitutional or political guarantees of individual and group rights against discrimination. Where the language of a major regional group has been denied recognition as a federal language, extreme bitterness and tension has resulted. Pakistan, Nigeria, India and Malaysia have provided examples of the intensity of resentment that can be aroused.

Strategies Adopted to Combat Disintegration

Once stress within a federation has reached a certain level, the issue of the appropriate strategy to combat it usually comes to the fore. Broadly speaking, in this sort of situation one of two alternative strategies has been attempted. One is to reinforce the strength and power of the federal government in order to resist disintegration and to hold the federation together. Such a strategy which in effect attempted to impose unity clearly failed in Pakistan, in Nigeria and in Malaysia (in relation to Singapore). An alternative strategy is to attempt to accommodate regional pressures by emphasizing further devolution. Such a strategy when carried out without any attempt to generate at the same time a focus of loyalty to the federation also has generally failed, as exemplified by the disintegrations of the West Indies Federation, the Federation of Rhodesia and Nyasaland and Czechoslovakia. It would appear from these examples that where the *sole* focus has been exclusively on one or other of these two strategies this has failed. Other cases where secession movements have been successfully countered suggest that what is required is a strategy that combines *both* efforts to strengthen a federal focus of loyalty *and* an accommodation of the major concerns of disaffected regional groups.

Polarizing Political Processes

The preceding survey indicates that there is no single condition, institutional arrangement or strategy that has by itself generated stress or led to disintegration in federations. In each case crises have been the product of a cumulative combination of factors. What does appear to be common is the resulting development of processes of a polarizing character. Where different kinds of social cleavages have reinforced each other, federal institutions have been unable to moderate or have even exacerbated these cleavages, political strategies have involved an emphasis upon either federal unity at the expense of regional accommodation or regional accommodation at the expense of federal unity, and negotiations have repeatedly failed to produce solutions, there has usually resulted a decline in the support for compromise and a cumulative political polarization within the federation. In such situations, political conflict has usually taken on the character of a contest with very high stakes in which each side becomes convinced that only one side can win and at the expense of the other. Once such a situation of emotional confrontation and mounting frenzy has developed, it has often taken only a relatively insignificant incident to trigger an act of unilateral secession or expulsion resulting in civil war or the disintegration of the federation.

11.3 THE SPECIAL PROBLEM OF BICOMMUNAL FEDERATIONS

A set of cases worthy of special examination is that of federal systems and federations composed of only two constituent units. In the current Canadian context, the experience of bipolar federations and confederations is relevant because proposals have been advanced from time to time for converting Canada into a confederation composed of two units: Quebec and a nine-province federation of the "Rest of Canada." Among such proposals have been those advanced by the Parti Québécois for sovereignty-association (1979-80) and the tripartite proposal put forward jointly by the Parti Québécois, the Bloc Québécois, and the Action Democratique du Québec for sovereignty and partnership (1995). While Canada is currently a federation of ten provinces and two territories, the notion of a bipolar confederation draws its rationale from the bicommunal character of Canada as a country of French-speaking and English-speaking Canadians, each in a majority within a territorial area within Canada.

The experience of bipolar or dyadic federal systems elsewhere is, however, not encouraging. Pakistan prior to the secession of East Pakistan in 1971 and Czechoslovakia prior to its segregation in 1992 have provided examples of the difficulties which arise in bipolar federations. Another relevant case was the bipolar racial and ideological Malaysia-Singapore relationship within the Malaysian federation which culminated in Singapore's expulsion after only two years. All three of these cases resulted in the end in the splitting of these federations. Indeed the particular difficulties of dyadic federations and unions have generally been recognized.[26]

The problem within two-unit federations generally has been that insistence upon parity in all matters between the two units has usually tended to produce impasses and deadlocks. This is because there is no opportunity for shifting alliances and coalitions among the constituent units which is one of the ways in which multi-unit federations are able to resolve issues. Furthermore, since invariably one of the two units is less populous than the other (e.g. West Pakistan and Slovakia) that unit has usually been particularly conscious of the continuous need to insist upon equality of influence in federal policy making, while the larger unit (and in the case of Czechoslovakia, the wealthier one) has developed a sense of grievance over the constraints imposed upon it to accommodate the smaller unit. The resulting cumulatively intensifying bipolarity in these examples led ultimately to their terminal instability. Such tendencies would appear likely to be accentuated in a two-unit confederation, since it is a normal characteristic of confederations that each member unit possesses a veto on all major policy decisions in the confederation. The existence of mutual vetoes where there are only two units is likely to be a recipe for repeated impasses and deadlocks contributing to cumulatively sharpening frustrations. Thus, the application of the European Union Maastricht model, which despite its difficulties works for a confederation of 15 member states, is likely to be much less workable when applied to a confederation of two units.[27]

11.4 PROCESSES AND CONSEQUENCES OF DISINTEGRATION

While the constitutions of nearly all federations have explicitly or implicitly prohibited unilateral secession by member units, these constitutional restrictions have seldom prevented alienated regional groups from taking matters into their own hands and acting extraconstitutionally. Once a regional unit has declared its own unilateral secession, a federal government is faced with the dilemma whether it should enforce the constitution of the federation upon the unwilling region or simply accept the secession as a political fact even if unconstitutional. In the past most independent (i.e. non-colonial) federations have chosen the former course, fearing that once the secession of one member unit is accepted there would be nothing to prevent other member units from separating whenever they wished or at least using such a threat as a lever against the federal government. Consequently, in a number of cases the result of a unilateral declaration of secession has been a civil war in which the federal government has imposed continued federation successfully, e.g. United States (1861-65), Switzerland (1847) and Nigeria (1967-70), or unsuccessfully, e.g. Pakistan (1971) and Yugoslavia (1991-95). The breakup of the USSR also led to some incidences of violence, and within the successor Russian federation bitter fighting in Chechnia followed an attempt at secession. One interesting case which did not involve violence was that of Western Australia which, dissatisfied with her place in the federation, in 1933 voted by a majority in a referendum to secede from the Australian federation. The Australian federal government, however, stood firm and refused to implement the separation of Western Australia (as did the United Kingdom Parliament when subsequently petitioned by the state of Western Australia to permit secession). The federal government instead responded to the concerns and grievances of Western Australia by establishing a system of special financial assistance to claimant states based on advice by a Commonwealth Grants Commission instituted in 1933.

While secessions have usually been contested there have been some cases of peaceful secession from federations.[28] Two of these, which led ultimately to the disintegration of the West Indies Federation (1962) and the Federation of Rhodesia and Nyasaland (1963), occurred in colonial federations. In these cases it was the imperial government in the United Kingdom which not only accepted secession but held the ring to ensure that there was no violence. Among independent federations the only cases of peaceful separation during the past half century have been in Malaysia and Czechoslovakia. The former in 1965 was not really a case of unilateral secession but of unilateral expulsion by the federal government reacting to the troublesome political dynamics that had followed Singapore's inclusion in the Malaysian federation two years earlier. The Czechoslovakian separation which came into effect on 1 January 1993 represents the only peaceful secession to have taken place in a modern, highly integrated industrial society. This peaceful secession occurred largely because it was the climax of a gradual but accelerating process of polarization in which the regionally based political parties within each of the two units found it politically profitable to engage in mutual antagonism, conflict and disagreement, and ultimately to effect the breakup of the federation without an election or referendum on the issue.[29]

Elsewhere, the general experience has been that once the separation of one unit has been conceded, other regional units have raised similar demands which have led to further disintegration. This was the pattern both in the West Indies and in Rhodesia and Nyasaland. Moreover, resentments aroused at the time of separation or dissolution have tended to persist. They have discouraged for a considerable subsequent period the creation of a looser form of association between the separating territories, because whenever secession has occurred it has inevitably been accompanied by sharp political controversies which were not easily forgotten. Furthermore, the unscrambling of federations has required the allocation of assets and liabilities among successor states and rarely has this been achieved without adding further to the resentments felt by one or both sides. In this respect the least negative examples have been those of the expulsion of Singapore from Malaysia and the separation of Czechoslovakia. Yet in both cases, despite professions about the desirability of continued economic linkages after separation, in practice for a considerable subsequent period economic ties fell far below expectations. Generally it is clear that the separation of units from federations, even in the few cases where it has been managed peacefully, has exacted a high price in economic costs, diplomatic and defensive ineffectiveness, and lasting bitterness between the groups involved.

Chapter 12

Conclusions

12.1 CANADA IN COMPARATIVE PERSPECTIVE

On the basis of this study we may summarize the Canadian federation in comparative perspective to the various other federations considered.

As a federation Canada's bilingual and multicultural character places it more in the category of such federations as Switzerland, India, Malaysia, Belgium and Spain where federation was adopted to accommodate and reconcile territorial diversity within a fundamentally multilingual and multicultural society. In this respect Canada differs from such federations as the United States, Australia, Austria and Germany with their more homogeneous societies, although valuable lessons can also be gained from examining the ways in which these examples have used federation to accommodate their internal diversity. Canada with its linguistic bipolarity shares some of the political characteristics of Belgium, Czechoslovakia and Pakistan (before 1971) although unlike the latter two it is composed of more than just two regional units of government. More than most federations, and like Australia, Canada's political dynamics are strongly influenced by the predominant political influence of two of its ten provinces because of their relatively large population.

In terms of the institutional characteristics, the form of the distribution of powers in Canada which generally allocates administrative responsibilities to the same order of government as that to which legislative responsibility is assigned (with the exception of criminal law) is similar to the United States and Australia. This contrasts with the greater constitutional devolution of administrative responsibility than legislative in Switzerland, Austria, Germany, India and Malaysia. However, in respect to concurrent jurisdiction, Canada is unlike the United States and Australia, and also Germany, India and Malaysia. The range of constitutionally assigned concurrent jurisdiction is very limited in Canada with most powers assigned exclusively to one level of government or the other. In this respect Canada is more similar to Belgium and Switzerland. With regard to the enumeration of provincial powers Canada is unlike the United States, Australia and Germany where the federal and concurrent jurisdiction is enumerated in the constitution but state powers consist of the unspecified residual jurisdiction. In Canada, as in India, Malaysia and Belgium the powers of the provinces are explicitly enumerated in the constitution, an arrangement which although originally centralist in intent has paradoxically over time better protected the scope of provincial powers when subjected to judicial review.

In terms of the distribution of revenues and expenditure responsibilities and efforts to ensure a balance of these, Canada has been more successful than most federations in preventing an undermining of the autonomy of the provinces. It has done so by depending less upon intergovernmental transfers as a percentage of total provincial revenues (Table 9) and by a heavier reliance upon unconditional transfers than other federations. While most federations have some form of equalization arrangement to deal with horizontal imbalances, Canada like Germany and Australia is among those with the most substantial equalization adjustments, although the Canadian equalization program, by contrast with Australia, focuses on equalizing revenue capacity and does not take account of variations in expenditure needs.

All federations have required intergovernmental processes and institutions to facilitate consultation and collaboration between their governments in the unavoidable areas of overlapping jurisdiction. These processes in Canada, as has been typical of all parliamentary federations, have taken on the character of "executive federalism," although this has not reached the formal level achieved in Australia or Germany.

While political asymmetry among the constituent units has been typical of all federations, Canada is among the minority of federations including Malaysia, India, Belgium and Spain where some degree of constitutional asymmetry has also been incorporated in order to reconcile varying regional pressures for autonomy. This has been a contentious issue in Canada during the constitutional deliberations of the past three decades, but the degree of constitutional asymmetry in Canada has not yet reached that in some other federations such as Malaysia or Spain.

We have noted that, as a result of the dual contemporary pressures, on the one hand, for federations to join larger supra-federal systems and, on the other, to give greater emphasis to the importance of local governments, federal arrangements elsewhere have often tended to take on a multi-tiered character. The Canadian federation is subject to these same pressures, of which its membership in the North American Free Trade Area is just one illustration. There is another respect in which the possibility of multi-tiered internal federal arrangements takes on a particular significant in Canada. That is the proposal to provide for Aboriginal aspirations to self-government through establishment of a "third order of government." In addressing the issue of Aboriginal self-government, the traditional characterization of federations as relating to only two constitutional levels of government and the interactions between them is likely to create barriers to an effective resolution. Recognition of the possibility of multi-tiered federal systems is likely to open up possible solutions to one of the fundamental political and constitutional issues facing Canada. But while multi-tiered federal systems provide new ways of resolving problems, it will also be necessary to guard against undue complexity that would undermine democratic accountability and introduce substantial additional costs.

The comparative degree of decentralization and non-centralization in different federations, although an issue often discussed in a loose way, is a complex issue to measure. Nevertheless, it is clear that although in some areas such as the regulation of the economic union Canada is the most decentralized, in a variety of other specific areas of jurisdiction Canada is less decentralized than some other federations. Overall Canada may be considered one of the more decentralized federations but not clearly the most.

In terms of the representative institutions of federal government, Canada belongs among those federations which have combined federation with parliamentary institutions. Indeed it was the first innovator in this respect. As in other parliamentary federations such as Australia, Austria, Germany, India, Malaysia, Belgium and Spain, this has affected processes for generating federal cohesion, inclusion of minority views in federal decision making and the executive-dominated nature of intergovernmental relations. Parliamentary government has also limited the potential role and influence of the Canadian Senate as a body representing regional viewpoints in federal decision making. The particular form of the "unreformed" Senate of Canada is unique, however, even among parliamentary federations in terms of its lack of political legitimacy as a body representing regional interests at the federal level. Because of the character of the Senate, but also the way in which the parliamentary system and the federal and provincial parties have operated, Canada provides less opportunity formally for representation and participation of provincial governments in federal decision making than virtually any other federation reviewed in this study. This in turn has contributed to the strength of the pressures for the processes of "executive federalism" in intergovernmental relations.

In its emphasis upon the supremacy of the constitution, upon judicial review as a major form of adjudication for intergovernmental disputes, and upon a variety of procedures for constitutional amendment (since 1982), most of which require provincial as well as federal involvement, Canada is typical of most federations. The inclusion of a Charter of Rights and Freedoms in the constitution in 1982 which includes not only *individual rights* but some specified *group rights* is similar to those other federations marked by sharp internal linguistic and cultural diversity, e.g. India, Malaysia and Belgium. It contrasts, however, with other more homogeneous federations which have either included a list of fundamental rights

confined to individual rights, e.g. Germany and the U.S.A., or no list of fundamental rights, e.g. Australia and Austria. Switzerland alone among multilingual
and multicultural federations has not set out fundamental individual and group
rights in the constitution, although in practice strong respect is paid to these.

No federation, other than the former USSR, has included a constitutional provision permitting unilateral secession by constituent regional units. Nor has any
formulated in advance the formal conditions required for secession. The Canadian constitution in this respect is typical of federations. Given the current
preoccupation in Canada with attempting to specify in advance the constitutionally valid terms for secession, it should be noted that in federations elsewhere
where secession has been attempted or succeeded, it has always in the end involved an overtly political rather than a validly constitutional act.

Examining the pathology of federations that have exhibited serious stresses or
even disintegration indicates that Canada is exhibiting some of the social and
political stresses and institutional failures found in other federations under strain.
Particularly serious is the tendency to increasing bipolarization. A key symptom
prior to disintegration of federations elsewhere has been the replacement in federal politics of political parties overarching regional interests by political parties
which are primarily regional in their focus. Canadian federal politics has since
1990 moved partly, but not yet all the way, in that direction.

12.2 IMPLICATIONS FOR THE FUTURE DEVELOPMENT OF THE CANADIAN FEDERATION

In drawing implications from this comparative analysis for the future development of the Canadian federation, we must keep in mind the comments at the
outset about the benefits and limits of comparisons with other federations. Comparisons do help to draw attention to crucial issues and to possible alternatives
illustrated by the experience of other federations. But we need also to recognize
the limits to the applicability of comparisons and particularly to the transferabil-
ity of institutions to differing circumstances and contexts. Above all it is important
to recognize that it is not simply in the examples of different institutional structures, but rather in coming to understand the way in which underlying social,
economic and political conditions, and federal institutions and political processes
have interacted with each other in federations that the comparisons may lead to
useful conclusions.

What we can learn from other federations that have succeeded is that even
more important than their formal structures has been the public acceptance of the
basic values and processes required for federal systems. These include the explicit recognition and accommodation of multiple identities and loyalties within
an overarching sense of shared purposes and objections. Efforts to deny or sup-
press the multiple identities within a diverse society have almost invariably led to

contention, secession or civil war. An essential element therefore in any federation encompassing a diverse society has been the acceptance of the value of diversity and of the possibility of multiple loyalties expressed through the establishment of constituent units of government with genuine autonomous self-rule over those matters most important to their distinct identity. At the same time equally important has been the recognition of the benefits derived from shared purposes and objectives within even a diverse society providing the basis for parallel processes of shared-rule.

This comparative study has made clear that within the general category of federal political systems and indeed within the more specific category of federations there has been a considerable variety in the patterns of social conditions accommodated and an enormous range in the institutional arrangements and political processes adopted. All these systems have attempted, many with considerable success, to combine elements of autonomous self-rule for the constituent units in certain matters and an overarching shared-rule in other matters in order to reconcile the desires for both distinctive diversity and united action. But the variations among them make it clear that there is no single pure ideal form of federation applicable everywhere. Federations have varied greatly in their institutional design and in their operation to meet their own particular conditions and context. The implication for the future development of the Canadian federation is that we should not be constrained to traditional arrangements or theories about federalism but should be ready to consider more imaginative and innovative ways of applying pragmatically the spirit of federalism as a way of combining unity and diversity. In this process we may be able to draw lessons or inspiration from practice in other federations, particularly in relation to identifying potential dangers to be averted, desirable objectives, and appropriate and inappropriate processes for achieving those objectives. But ultimately, while bearing these in mind, if the future development of the Canadian federation is to be effective and long-lasting, efforts will have to be directed at pragmatically accommodating the particular conditions and "realities" of Canada. Nevertheless, in the light of comparisons with other federations, it would appear that there is room in Canada within the framework of a federation for some rebalancing of federal and provincial jurisdictions involving the further decentralization of some functions in relation to specific matters and for improving the representation of regional inputs within the institutions of federal policy making.

If such is the case, a concluding word about the process by which the Canadian federation is adapted would seem to be in order. For thirty years proposals for a major constitutional restructuring have been debated by Canadians. To meet the concerns of those in Quebec and also of many Canadians elsewhere who desire neither the constitutional status quo nor separation, we have gone through four rounds of intense mega-constitutional debate. These rounds in 1968-71, 1976-82, 1987-90 and 1990-92, each aimed at seeking agreement on a comprehensive constitutional restructuring that would be a better alternative to either the status quo or separation. All that effort, however, has produced no lasting agreement on a satisfactory resolution. Indeed, it has heightened frustration. The 1992 referendum on the Charlottetown Consensus Report demonstrated conclusively just how difficult it is to get popular acceptance of comprehensive constitutional reform. Consequently, at the present time any suggestion of yet another round of constitutional negotiations is met by resistance and antipathy outside Quebec and by cynicism within Quebec. Thus, it appears, at least on the surface, that the prospects for finding the middle ground for future development have seriously eroded.

Is Canada therefore reduced, as some conclude, to the simple stark alternatives between an unchanging federation or Quebec independence? This is so only if we are misled into assuming that the only kind of significant change to the federal system is comprehensive constitutional change. Indeed, experience in many federations elsewhere, such as Switzerland, Australia, the United States and Germany, has indicated that attempts at major comprehensive constitutional reform have always proved extremely difficult and have usually failed. Instead substantial change and even transformation have been achieved in each of these federations by incremental piecemeal constitutional adjustment and even more by pragmatic political adaptation.[30]

Our own Canadian experiences bear this out. It has only been in the last thirty years that Canadians have become preoccupied with comprehensive constitutional change as the appropriate way of trying to resolve all our political problems. In the 115 years of our history as a federation before 1982 much adjustment in the directions of both decentralization and centralization were the product of political rather than constitutional action. During that period certain central powers like reservation, disallowance and the declaratory power fell into disuse. Also the increased prominence of the provinces on the one hand, and the finessing of the constitutional distribution of powers by Ottawa's use of its "spending power" on the other, both transformed the Canadian federation without resort to constitutional amendment. Furthermore, in recent decades far-reaching changes in the structure and operation of the Canadian federation have come through the impact of fiscal circumstances and the normal interactions of the policies of federal and provincial governments rather than through formal constitutional amendment.

Many of the basic present concerns of Canadians including those of Quebecers can be met by means other than formal constitutional amendment. Indeed, the current need to redefine federal-provincial programs and shared-cost agreements in response to fiscal circumstances will unavoidably reshape the Canadian federation fundamentally in the direction of decentralization. Considerable progress on many issues, including the much needed rebalancing of federal and provincial roles and the reduction, where appropriate, of unnecessary duplication, can be made by means of ordinary legislative and administrative action and by intergovernmental agreements. What is more, such incremental nonconstitutional adaptation may be much easier to achieve when the higher stake deliberations of mega-constitutional politics are avoided. The history of most federations, including our own, indicates that federations are essentially a pragmatically evolving rather than static form of government. Failure to respond to changing conditions and needs is likely to become a cumulatively intense source of stress, but the lesson from other federations is that effective response is more likely to be achieved by incremental political adaptation supplemented where necessary by specific constitutional adjustments rather than by efforts at comprehensive constitutional transformation.

Appendix A

The Distribution of Powers and Functions in Federations: A Comparative Overview

The purpose of this appendix is to provide a comparative overview of the constitutional distribution of powers in the 12 federations upon which this study focuses. The table is a revised version of tables which were previously published in Ronald L. Watts, *Multicultural Societies and Federalism* (Ottawa: Information Canada, 1970), pp. 96-101 and Dwight Herperger, *Distribution of Powers and Functions in Federal Systems* (Ottawa: Minister of Supply and Services, 1991), pp. 43-48. Information in this table is based on a reading of constitutional texts, academic interpretive texts and other sources. The tables indicate whether legislative authority for a subject matter is Federal (F), State (S) or Concurrent (C). Where different aspects of a matter are assigned exclusively to the federal and to the state governments this is indicated by the notation FS. The legend at the bottom of each page explains the notations for variations or exceptions to these standard classifications. A space left blank indicates that the matter is not explicitly referred to in the constitution or that the power to legislate in that area rests with the residual authority (indicated in the first line of the table). The content and allocation of some subjects are often more complex than might appear from the table, and reference to the constitutional documents themselves should be made for greater detail.

The Distribution of Powers and Functions in Federal Systems: A Comparative Overview

	Canada (1867)	United States (1789)	Switzerland (1848)	Australia (1901)	Germany (1949)	Austria (1929)	India (1950)	Malaysia (1963)	Belgium (1993)	Spain (1978)	Czechoslovakia (1968)	Pakistan (1962)
BASIC FEATURES												
Residual Power	F	S	S	S	S	S	F	S	F	FS*	S	S
Enumeration of State Powers	YES	NO	NO	NO	YES	YES	YES	YES	YES[a]	YES	NO	NO
Delegation of Legislative Authority	NO	NO	NO	YES	NO	NO	YES	YES		YES		YES
SCOPE OF POWERS												
Finance and Fiscal Relations												
Taxation												
Customs/Excise	F	F/C	F	F	F	F	F/FS	F[a]	C	F	F	F
Corporate	FS	C	F	C	C†	F	F	F	C	F	F	F
Personal Income	FS	C	FS	C	C†	F	FS	F	C	FS[a]	F	FS
Sales	FS	C	F	C	C†	F	FS	F[a]	C	F	S	F
Other									Sr	FS[a]		
Equalization	F		F		FS				F		F	
Debt and Borrowing												
Public Debt of the Federation	F	F	F	F	F	F	F	F	F	F	F	F
Foreign Borrowing	FS	FS	FS	C	FS	F	F	F	FScr	FS	FS	FS
Domestic Borrowing	FS	FS	FS	C	FS		FS	FS	FScr	FS	FS	FS

Legend:

F = federal power

S = state (provincial/canton/Länd/autonomous community)

C = concurrent power (federal paramountcy except where denoted C* which denotes provincial paramountcy)

c = "Community" power

r = "Regional" power

* = 5 of the 17 sub-national orders of government retain residual powers, for the others the residual powers are federal

[a] = asymmetrical application of powers

† = federal legislation in this field administered by the states

The Distribution of Powers and Functions *(continued)*

	Canada (1867)	United States (1789)	Switzerland (1848)	Australia (1901)	Germany (1949)	Austria (1929)	India (1950)	Malaysia (1963)	Belgium (1993)	Spain (1978)	Czechoslovakia (1968)	Pakistan (1962)
International Relations												
Defence	F	FS	F		F	F	F	F	F	F	F	F
Treaty Implementation	F(1)	F	F	FS	F	F	F	F	F	F	F	F
Citizenship	F	F	F*	F	FS	F(1)	F(2)	F(2)S	ScrF	F	F	F(2)
Immigration (into federation)	C	C	C	C	FC†	FS†	F	F^a	F	F	F	F
Immigration (between regions)					C†	F	F	C^a				
Functioning of Economic Union												
"Trade and Commerce"	F	F	F	F	C†	F	F	F	Sc	F	F	F
External Trade	F	F	F	C			F	F^a	Sr	F	C	F
Inter-state Trade	F	F	F	C			F	F^a				F
Intra-state Trade	S	S		S			SC	F^a				
Currency	FS(3)	F	F	F	F	F	F	F	F	F	F	F
Banking	F	C	F	C	C†	F	F	F	F	F	C	FS
Bankruptcy	F	FS		C		F	C	F	F	F		
Insurance	FS	FS	FS	C		F	F	F^a	F	F		FS

Legend:

F = federal power

S = state (provincial/canton/Länd)

C = concurrent power (federal paramountcy except where denoted C^s which denotes provincial paramountcy)

c = "Community" power

r = "Regional" power

^{a} = asymmetrical application of powers

† = federal legislation in this field administered by the states

This page:

(1) = requires implementing legislation or consent of provincial or state governments

(2) = requires consultation (non-binding of state governments)

(3) = banking is exclusively federal but savings and credit unions are provincial

* = cantonal governments are free to set standards within the limits imposed by federal legislation

The Distribution of Powers and Functions *(continued)*

	Canada (1867)	United States (1789)	Switzerland (1848)	Australia (1901)	Germany (1949)	Austria (1929)	India (1950)	Malaysia (1963)	Belgium (1993)	Spain (1978)	Czechoslovakia (1968)	Pakistan (1962)
Transportation and Communications												
Roads and Bridges	S	FS	FS	FS	FC†	FS	FS	F	Sr	SF		
Railways	FS	FS	F	FS	C†	F	F	FS	F	S		S
Air	F	F	F	FS	FC†	F	F	Fª	Sr	SF		F
Telecommunications	FS	FS	F	C	F	F	F	F	F	F	C	F
Postal Services	F	F	F	C	F	F	F	F	F	F	C	F
Broadcasting	F	F	F	C	FC†	F	F	F	Sc	F	C	F
Agriculture and Resources												
Agriculture	C	S	FS	SC	C†	F†	SC	SCª	Sr	S	C	
Fisheries	FS	S		FS	C†		FS	FS	Sr	S*F		FS
Mineral Resources	FS	S		S		F	FS	FS	Sr	F	F	
Nuclear Energy	F	FS	F	C	C	F	F		F	F		F

Legend:

F = federal power

S = state (provincial/canton/Länd)

C = concurrent power (federal paramountcy except where denoted Cˢ which denotes provincial paramountcy)

c = "Community" power

r = "Regional" power

ª = asymmetrical application of powers

* = fishing in inland waters

† = federal legislation in this field administered by the states

Note: Italics denote *de facto* distribution of powers and functions

The Distribution of Powers and Functions *(continued)*

	Canada (1867)	United States (1789)	Switzerland (1848)	Australia (1901)	Germany (1949)	Austria (1929)	India (1950)	Malaysia (1963)	Belgium (1993)	Spain (1978)	Czechoslovakia (1968)	Pakistan (1962)
Social Affairs												
Education and Research												
Primary and Secondary Education	S	S	C†S	S	S	FS	CS	F[a]	Sc	FS*	S	
Postsecondary Education	S	FS	FC†S	FS	C†**	F	FCS	F[a]	Sc	F		
Research and Development		FS	C†	FS	C†	FS	FCS	F[a]	FSc			FS
Health Services						F		F				
Hospitals	SF	SF	S	FS	C†	C†	S	F[a]	Sc	FS*		
Public Health and Sanitation	S	S	C†	S		FS	S	FC	Sc	S		
Labour and Social Services								F			C	
Unemployment Insurance	F	FS	C†	C	C†	F	S	F[a]	F	F		
Income Security	FS		FC	C	C†	F	CS	F[a]	F	F		
Social Services	SF	SF	C†	C	C†	S	CS	C	Sc	FS		C
Pensions	C[s]	C	C†	C	F	F	C	F[a]S	F	F	F	FS

Legend:

F = federal power

S = state (provincial/canton/Länd)

C = concurrent power (federal paramountcy except where denoted C[s] which denotes provincial paramountcy)

c = "Community" power

r = "Regional" power

[a] = asymmetrical application of powers

* = 6 of the 17 sub-national orders of government have jurisdiction over education and health

** = enumerated as a framework legislation jurisdiction whereby the federal government may enact general principles only

† = federal legislation in this field administered by the states

Note: Italics denote *de facto* distribution of powers and functions

The Distribution of Powers and Functions (continued)

	Canada (1867)	United States (1789)	Switzerland (1848)	Australia (1901)	Germany (1949)	Austria (1929)	India (1950)	Malaysia (1963)	Belgium (1993)	Spain (1978)	Czechoslovakia (1968)	Pakistan (1962)
Law and Security												
Civil Law	S	S	F	FS	C†	FS*	C	F[a]S	F	F		
Criminal Law	F	S	F	S	C†	FS*	C	F				
Organization of Courts	FS	FS	S	FS	C†	F	FS	F[a]				FS
Internal Security (police)	FS	FS	S	SF	C†S	FS	FS	F	F	FS[a]	C	S
Prisons	FS	FS	S	S	S	F	S	F		F		
Other Matters												
Language	FS		S				FS	F	FSc	FS		
Culture	FS		C†				FS	FS	Sc	FCS[a]	S	
Aboriginal Affairs	F	F		C				C				
Environment	FS	FS	C†	FS	C†	FS	FS	F[a]	Sr	C		
Municipal Affairs	S	S	S	S	S	S	S	F[a]S	FSr	FS		

Legend:

F = federal power

S = state (provincial/canton/Länd)

C = concurrent power (federal paramountcy except where denoted C* which denotes provincial paramountcy)

c = "Community" power

r = "Regional" power

[a] = asymmetrical application of powers

† = federal legislation in this field administered by the states

* = states may legislate in the fields of criminal and civil law if necessary to dispose of an item within the scope of their legislative competence (Article 15, paragraph 9)

Notes

1. Daniel J. Elazar, *Federalism: an Overview*, (Pretoria:HSRC, 1995), p. 19.

2. E.A. Freeman, *History of Federal Government in Greece and Italy*, ed. by J.B. Bury, (London and New York: Macmillan and Co., 1893).

3. Ibid.; Elazar, *Federalism*, p. 20.

4. Thomas J. Courchene, "Glocalization: The Regional/International Interface," *Canadian Journal of Regional Science*, 18:1 (Spring 1995): 1-20.

5. To complicate the picture further, Benelux, one of whose members is itself a federation (Belgium), represents a confederation within the wider confederal European Union.

6. Elazar, *Federalism,* 2-7, 16, and Daniel J. Elazar, ed., *Federal Systems of the World*, 2nd ed. (Harlow: Longman Group Limited, 1994), xvi.

7. These tables have been adapted from Elazar, *Federalism*.

8. Peter M. Leslie, *The Maastricht Model: A Canadian Perspective on the European Union* (Kingston: Institute of Intergovernmental Relations, Queen's University, Research Paper No. 33, 1996).

9. For a full analysis see Robert A. Young, *The Breakup of Czechoslovakia* (Kingston: Institute of Intergovernmental Relations, Queen's University, Research Paper No. 32, 1994).

10. See for instance, K.C. Wheare, *Federal Government*, 4th ed., (London: Oxford University Press, 1963), p. 14.

11. The figures for Canada in this section are derived from the Canada Tax Foundation, *Provincial and Municipal Finances* (1991).

12. See Douglas M. Brown, *Equalization on the Basis of Need in Canada* (Kingston: Institute of Intergovernmental Relations, Queen's University, Reflections Paper No. 15, 1996).

13. Richard M. Bird, "A Comparative Perspective on Federal Finance" in Keith G. Banting, Douglas M. Brown, Thomas J. Courchene, eds., *The Future of Fiscal Federalism* (Kingston: School of Policy Studies, Institute of Intergovernmental Relations, John Deutsch Institute for the Study of Economic Policy, Queen's University, 1994), pp. 304-5

14. Bird, "A Comparative Perspective," 305.

15. For a fuller study of this phenomenon see Ronald L. Watts, *Executive Federalism: A Comparative Analysis* (Kingston: Institute of Intergovernmental Relations, Queen's University, Research Paper No. 20, 1989).

16. For an example of such a proposal in Canada see Thomas J. Courchene, *ACCESS: A Convention on the Canadian Economic and Social Systems* (a working paper prepared for the Ministry of Intergovernmental Affairs, Government of Ontario, 1996).

17. F. Scharpf, "The Joint Decision Trap: Lessons from German Federalism and European Integration," *Public Administration*, 66 (autumn 1988): 238-78.

18. Albert Breton, "Supplementary Statement," in Royal Commission on the Economic Union and Development Prospects for Canada, MacDonald Commission, *Report*, Vol. 3, (Ottawa: Supply and Services Canada, 1985), pp. 486-526.

19. Daniel J. Elazar, *Exploring Federalism* (Tuscaloosa: University of Alabama Press, 1987), pp. 34-36.

20. Ronald L. Watts, *New Federations: Experiments in the Commonwealth* (Oxford: Clarendon Press, 1966), p. 375.

21. Morton Grodzins, "The Federal System," A. Wildavsky, ed., in *American Federalism in Comparative Perspective* (Boston: Little Brown, 1967), p. 257.

22. Kenneth D. McRae, *Conflict and Compromise in Multilingual Societies: Switzerland* (Waterloo: Wilfrid Laurier University Press, 1983), p. 21.

23. Ibid., 122.

24. J.R. Pennock, "Federal and Unitary Government — Disharmony and Reliability," *Behavioral Science*, 4: 2 (1959): 147-57: Martin Landau, "Federalism, Redundancy and System Reliability," *Publius: The Journal of Federalism*, 3: 2 (1973): 173-95.

25. See, for instance, Thomas Franck, *Why Federations Fail: An Inquiry into the Requisites for a Successful Federation* (New York: New York University Press, 1966); Ronald L. Watts, "The Survival and Disintegration of Federations," in R. Simeon, ed., *Must Canada Fail?* (Montreal: McGill-Queen's Press, 1977), 42-60; Ursula K. Hicks, *Federalism: Failure and Success: A Comparative Study* (London: Macmillan, 1978); Robert A. Young, *The Secession of Quebec and the Future of Canada* (Montreal and Kingston: McGill-Queen's Press, 1995), chapters 10 and 11.

26. See, for instance, Ivo Duchacek, "Dyadic Federations and Confederations," *Publius: The Journal of Federalism*, 18: 2 (1988): 5-31.

27. Peter M. Leslie, *The Maastricht Model*.

28. For an analysis of these cases in detail see Young, *The Secession of Quebec,* chapters 10 and 11; and Young, *The Breakup of Czechoslovakia*.

29. Young, *The Breakup of Czechoslovakia*, p. 145.

30. This was a major theme that emerged from the international conference on "Redesigning the State: The Politics of Mega Constitutional Change" held at the Australian National University in Canberra, 27-29 July 1994.

Selected Readings

Bakvis, Herman and William M. Chandler, eds., *Federalism and the Role of the State* (Toronto: University of Toronto Press, 1987).

Bird, Richard A., *Federal Finance in Comparative Perspective* (Toronto: Canadian Tax Foundation, 1986).

_____, "A Comparative Perspective on Federal Finance," in K.G. Banting, D.M. Brown, T.J. Courchene, eds., *The Future of Fiscal Federalism* (Kingston: School of Policy Studies, Institute of Intergovernmental Relations, John Deutsch Institute for the Study of Economic Policy, Queen's University, 1994), pp. 293-322.

Brown-John, C. Lloyd, ed., *Centralizing and Decentralizing Trends in Federal States* (London: University Press of America, 1988).

Burgess, Michael and Alain-G. Gagnon, eds., *Comparative Federalism and Federation: Competing Trends and Future Directions* (Hemel Hempstead: Harvester Wheatsheaf, 1993).

De Villiers, Bertus, ed., *Evaluating Federal Systems* (Cape Town: Jutta & Co., 1994).

Duchacek, Ivo, *Comparative Federalism: The Territorial Dimension of Politics*, rev. ed. (Lanham: University Press of America, 1987).

Elazar, Daniel J. *Exploring Federalism* (Tuscaloosa, AL: University of Alabama Press, 1987).

_____, ed., *Federal Systems of the World: A Handbook of Federal, Confederal and Autonomy Arrangements*, 2nd ed., (Harlow: Longman Group Limited, 1994).

_____, *Federalism: an Overview* (Pretoria: HSRC, 1995).

_____, *Federalism and the Way to Peace* (Kingston: Institute of Intergovernmental Relations, Queen's University, 1994).

Forsyth, Murray, *Unions of States: The Theory and Practice of Confederation* (Leicester: Leicester University Press, 1981).

_____, ed., *Federalism and Nationalism* (Leicester: Leicester University Press, 1989).

Friedrich, Carl J. *Trends of Federalism in Theory and Practice* (New York: Praeger, 1968).

Hamilton, Alexander, John Jay and James Madison, *The Federalist* (1788).

Hicks, Ursula K., *Federalism: Failure and Success: A Comparative Study* (London: Macmillan, 1978).

Herperger, Dwight, *Distribution of Powers and Functions in Federal Systems* (Ottawa: Minister of Supply and Services Canada, 1991).

King, Preston, *Federalism and Federation* (London: Croom Helm, 1982).

Lalande, Gilles, *In Defence of Federalism: The View from Quebec* (Toronto: McClelland and Stewart, 1978).

Landau, Martin, "Federalism, Redundancy and System Reliability," *Publius: The Journal of Federalism*, 3:2 (1973):173-195.

Olson, David M. and C.E.S. Franks, eds., *Representation and Policy Formation in Federal Systems* (Berkeley: Institute of Governmental Studies Press, 1993).

Ostrom, Vincent, "Can Federalism Make a Difference," *Publius: The Journal of Federalism*, 3:3 (1974):197-238.

Pennock, J.R., "Federal and Unitary Government — Disharmony and Reliability," *Behavioural Science*, 4:2 (1959):147-157.

Riker, William H., "Federalism," in Fred I. Greenstein and Nelson W. Polsby, eds., *Handbook of Political Science: Governmental Institutions and Processes*, Vol. 5, (Reading, Mass: Addison Wesley, 1975).

Sawer, Geoffrey, *Modern Federalism* (London: CA Watts, 1969).

Smiley, Donald V. and Ronald L. Watts, *Intrastate Federalism in Canada* (Toronto: University of Toronto Press, 1985), ch. 4.

Watts, Ronald L., *New Federations: Experiments in the Commonwealth* (Oxford: Clarendon Press, 1966).

_____, *Multicultural Societies and Federalism,* Studies of the Royal Commission on Bilingualism and Biculturalism, No. 8, (Ottawa: Information Canada, 1970).

_____, *Executive Federalism: A Comparative Analysis* (Kingston: Institute of Intergovernmental Relations, Queen's University, 1989).

Wheare, K.C. *Federal Government*, 4th ed. (London: Oxford University Press, 1963).

Young, Robert A., *The Secession of Quebec and the Future of Canada* (Montreal & Kingston: McGill-Queen's University Press, 1995), chs. 10 and 11.